CHURCH PLANTING
for a
GREATER HARVEST

A COMPREHENSIVE GUIDE

WHY NEW CHURCHES ARE NEEDED
HOW TO LAY THE SPIRITUAL AND PRACTICAL GROUNDWORK
HOW NEW CHURCHES CAN HELP EXISTING CHURCHES GROW
WAYS TO TARGET AND ATTRACT THE PEOPLE YOU WANT TO REACH
TWELVE PROVEN METHODS TO HELP YOU GET STARTED

C. PETER WAGNER

Regal Books
A Division of Gospel Light
Ventura, California, U.S.A.

Published by Regal Books
A Division of Gospel Light
Ventura, California, U.S.A.
Printed in U.S.A.

Regal Books is a ministry of Gospel Light, an evangelical Christian publisher dedicated to serving the local church. We believe God's vision for
Gospel Light is to provide church leaders with biblical, user-friendly mate-
rials that will help them evangelize, disciple and minister to children, youth
and families.

It is our prayer that this Regal Book will help you discover biblical truth
for your own life and help you meet the needs of others. May God rich-
ly bless you.

*For a free catalog of resources from Regal Books/Gospel Light please contact
your Christian supplier or call* 1-800-4-GOSPEL.

Library of Congress Cataloging-in-Publication Data

Wagner, C. Peter.
Church planting for a greater harvest: A comprehensive guide / C. Peter
Wagner.
p. cm.
Includes bibliographical references and index.
ISBN 0-8307-1435-9
1. Church development, New. 2. Church growth. I. Title.
BV652.24.W34   1990
254'.1—dc20   90-45513
                                                                     CIP

7 8 9 10 11 12 13 14 15 16 17 18 19 / X3 / KP / 99 98 97 96

Rights for publishing this book in other languages are contracted by Gospel
Literature International (GLINT). GLINT also provides technical help for the
adaptation, translation, and publishing of Bible study resources and books in
scores of languages worldwide. For further information, contact GLINT, Post
Office Box 4060, Ontario, California, 91761-1003, U.S.A., or the publisher.

To Doris in celebration of 40 years of
partnership in life and ministry.

CONTENTS

91733

INTRODUCTION

This book is intended to do three things:

1. Motivate church leaders to give the ministry of planting new churches a higher place on their personal and institutional agendas.

2. Show them the different ways and means available to vigorously multiply churches across the land.

3. Provide some of the tools necessary to make it happen.

We live in a time when general interest in church planting is higher than it has been since the 1950s. While some denominations continued to plant new churches and thereby have grown during the last 40 years, others have virtually eliminated that ministry with the exception of a new church here and there or a cluster of ethnic minority churches. They have been paying the price.

Now the climate is changing. Denominational headquarters are adding church planting desks. Motivational material is appearing in denominational publications. Training programs for church planters are being developed.

I have been working on the subject of church planting for over 10 years. When my studies of church growth here in the United States and around the world led me to the conclusion that the most effective evangelistic method under heaven was planting new churches, I began to ask how it was being taught in my own institution. I examined the Fuller Theological Seminary curriculum and found no courses on church planting. When I looked further, I discovered that the subject had not been taught since the seminary was founded in the late 1940s. Since none of the faculty of the School of Theology was planning to introduce a course on church planting, I decided to try it in our School of World Mission in the late 1970s. It proved to be a popular elective, and I have had the privilege of training hundreds and hundreds of Fuller students, many of whom have subsequently planted healthy churches. The course is still offered.

As word of the course began to circulate, several pastors told me that they wanted the training, but could not come to Fuller for a quarter of residence. To help meet the need, the Charles E. Fuller Institute of Evangelism and Church Growth began to offer a public "How to Plant a Church" seminar in 1983. From 1983 to 1989 the seminar was offered 16 times and drew 5,000 participants. Scores of denominational executives have attended the seminar (some several times), learned how to present the material, adapted it to their own denominational contexts, and are now holding training seminars within their own spheres of influence. This is a significant reason why interest in planting new churches is increasing so rapidly in our day.

Because of this shift, the seminar has now been discontinued. This helped me decide to put what I had been researching and teaching for over a decade into this book and thereby make it available for church planters, supervisors of church planters, trainers of church planters, denominational executives, local church pastors, lay leaders, and missionaries. As you read, you will find not only an up-to-date textbook on church planting but also a helpful summary of church growth principles in general.

You will also find a strong emphasis on the spiritual dimensions of church growth and church planting. As we have moved through the '80s and now enter the '90s, God continues to show us that the real battle for any form of the extension of the kingdom of God is spiritual. "Unless the Lord builds the house, they labor in vain who build it" (Ps. 127:1, *NKJV*). I believe that more and more we will see the technology that we have been developing over the years being wedded to fresh power from the Holy Spirit to carry us into the greatest era of harvest the world has ever seen.

I pray that God will allow me to be a part of it, and I pray the same for you.

1
CHURCH GROWTH AND CHURCH PLANTING

I begin this book with a categorical statement that will seem bold and brash to some at first sight, even though it has been well substantiated by research over the past two or three decades: *The single most effective evangelistic methodology under heaven is planting new churches.*

I have said it once, and I will say it many more times before this book is finished. This axiom is simple, but it is not simplistic. It applies monoculturally and cross culturally. It holds true, as we will see later on, both on new ground and on old ground. Some Christian leaders so badly wish it weren't true that when they aren't attempting to deny it, they are ignoring it. But one of the tragic results of that attitude is that many of the mainline denominations in America now find themselves in a serious membership decline that has continued unbroken for over 25 years.

Many books on evangelism (perhaps 98 percent) say nothing about church planting at all as an evangelistic methodology. Granted, many of them are written to promote personal soul winning, and I applaud them. It is true that the average Christian in the pew and the average pastor give little, if any, thought to planting new churches. Winning their friends and relatives to Christ and ministering in their own local congregations is all they can handle. But that is the small picture. Those who see the big picture see it differently, or at least they should if they are committed to the spread of the kingdom of God throughout their city or their region or the world. Evangelizing people by persuading them to go through the "Four Spiritual Laws" or come forward in a large crusade is excellent. But if these people who so express their desire to follow Jesus are not subsequently folded into a local congregation, their decision may turn out to be nothing more than a gesture. They never become disciples of Jesus Christ.

Not to make an explicit connection between evangelism and the local church is a strategic blunder. As the number of individuals who are evangelized increases, so also must the number of churches and the variety of churches. The more harvest God gives us, the more barns and silos and grain elevators are needed. In any given geographical area, the Christian community will grow or decline according to the degree of effort given to planting new churches.

GROWING DENOMINATIONS PLANT CHURCHES

While some denominations have been declining in the United States, other denominations in the same country through the same period of time have been growing vigorously. Without exception, the growing denominations have been those that stress church planting. The leaders of these denominations know that church planting is a central key to their growth, so not only do they believe it themselves, but they see to it that their pastors and lay leaders also believe it. They go to great pains to communicate the challenge of church planting throughout their constituency.

They are successful in keeping church planting high on the agendas of their people across the board.

Church of the Nazarene
My files are bulging with samples of well-produced communication pieces that some of the growing denominations have developed. My friends in the Church of the Nazarene,

Without exception, the growing denominations have been those that stress church planting.

for example, have sent me many excellent booklets, pamphlets, flyers, and tabloids. I love one of their four-page flyers dressed up with pleasing colors, cute caricatures, artistic layout and a simple message: "How a Church Is Born." It says that a birth implies "loving parents, anticipation, pain, attending physicians, tender care." It outlines seven steps in the church birth process. Then my friend, Raymond W. Hurn, who wrote it, makes this telling observation: "Few, if any parents, would ever say it was not worth the time, trouble, or expense to give birth to the infant and watch it grow through childhood and adolescence into adulthood."

How true this is. J. Ted Holstein, the District Superintendent of the Nazarene Wisconsin District, did a thorough study of church growth in his district. Using Sunday School attendance as a measuring stick, he found that in the six years from 1973 to 1979 attendance had declined from about 2,500 to about 2,050. He saw the danger sign and called in church planters. The graph of growth immediately turned around. If he had not planted new churches, the attendance six years later in 1985 would have been about 1,900. Actually, with the new churches, it was 2,250.

There is scarcely a district or a conference or a presbytery or a diocese or a whole national denomination that could not turn their graph of growth around by doing what Ted Holstein did in Wisconsin. I can't make a guarantee, but I will say that if you as a denominational leader make a conscientious effort to put the principles of this book into action and your growth does not turn around, I'll personally refund to you the price of this book!

Assemblies of God

Year after year one of the fastest growing denominations in the United States has been the Assemblies of God. They have constantly held church planting high. Articles and motivational pieces on church planting regularly appear in their clergy journal, *Advance*. In their family magazine, *Pentecostal Evangel*, they use state-of-the-art graphics to excite their people about new churches. They let them know, for example, that while in California there is only one Assembly of God for every 26,000 people, in Arkansas there is one for every 5,000. Their message? "New congregations become part of the vanguard, God's elite task force, which marches in advance in world conquest for Christ."

As they moved into the crucial decade of the 1990s the Assemblies of God had no intention of allowing their vigorous growth rate to weaken. In 1988 their Executive Presbytery signed a declaration designating the 1990s as the Decade of Harvest, and set the following goals: "To enlist 1 million prayer partners; to reach and win 5 million persons to Christ; to train and disciple 20,000 persons for ministry; *to establish 5,000 new churches.*"

Working from a base of slightly over 12,000 churches, this is indeed a bold goal. They are projecting an increase of around 40 percent. What would happen to Christianity in America if each of our historic mainline denominations projected only a half or a quarter that many? Why not? The unbelievers who are to be won to Christ could just as well be Methodists or Presbyterians or Lutherans or Episcopalians as they could be Pentecostals. Whoever gets there first and shows them how the gospel of Jesus Christ can meet their deepest needs will be able to win them. And the evidence is now in that an extremely effective way of making this happen is to plant new churches.

But some might object by saying that the Assemblies of God are taking too big a risk to announce such a bold goal. Suppose they don't make it? All right, suppose they don't. Suppose they end the decade with only 2,500 or 3,000 new churches? They're still better off than they would have been without making the effort. And even then they will end up with a net gain of more churches in a decade than many U.S. denominations many times larger will have gained in three or four decades combined.

Some Others

It is not by accident that the Southern Baptists have become the largest Protestant denomination in America. One of their secrets is that they constantly invest substantial resources of personnel and finances in church planting on all levels from local congregations to associations to state conventions to their Home Mission Board in Atlanta. Although they will be the first to admit they don't do it enough, every year they strive to start more new churches or church-type missions than the previous year. Much of what I have learned about church planting I have learned from Southern Baptists.

I am so excited about vigorous efforts for church planting that I keep my own informal record book on some of them. For example, I think the Church of God (Cleveland) set a record on May 5, 1985, when they organized 28 new churches in Alabama in one day. But the record was broken on Easter Sunday in 1987 when the Christian and Missionary Alliance organized 101 on the same day with an average attendance of 88. This means that over 8,000 people were in Alliance churches that Sunday who were not there the Sunday before. The Alliance leaders got so enthusiastic after this that they announced "1,000 more by '94!" Of course both the Church of God (Cleveland) and the Christian and Missionary Alliance have been among America's most rapidly growing denominations.

SEMINARY STUDENTS CAN DO IT

I hope it doesn't take you as long as it took me to discover that students right out of seminary are among those who have the highest potential for being successful church planters.

I had been teaching church growth in Fuller Seminary for several years. I had discovered that *planting new churches is the most effective evangelistic method under heaven.* Then I woke up one day to the realization that in the whole history of Fuller Seminary no course in church planting had been introduced into the curriculum. I checked around to see if anyone was planning on starting such a course, and when I found they weren't, I decided to do it myself. I knew very little about it when I started, but one thing I thought I knew was that the best church planters would probably be experienced pastors who had served several parishes and who had accumulated the wisdom and maturity to do it well.

Wrong!

Not that some fitting this description wouldn't make good church planters because they do. However, experienced pastors do not turn out to be the most likely talent pool. Younger people who still have more options and more flexibility are considerably more likely to do well. Since I began challenging my own students to plant churches, I have seen several each year go through a change in their career planning. When I describe some of the advantages of starting from scratch rather then inheriting a collection of someone else's problems in an existing parish, some take me up on it and start churches.

One of my greatest encouragements as I was coming to realize how valuable seminary students were for church planting was my close friendship with Rick Warren, a young Southern Baptist graduate of Southwestern Baptist Theological Seminary in Fort Worth. Rick packed his family into a car with a U-Haul trailer and set out in 1980 to plant a church in south Orange County, California. He announced his goal as a church of 20,000 by the year 2020 and planting a new church each year on the way. Could a seminary student do it? By 1989 his attendance was running between 4,000 and 5,000, right on the curve toward 20,000. And instead of starting nine new churches, he had started 14. For years Rick Warren has helped me teach my church planting course at Fuller and he has inspired and challenged scores of students to step out and risk it for God.

The Clergy Surplus

One of the severe problems that many of the traditional denominations have been facing is a surplus of ordained clergy. The number of their existing churches has been declining, but their seminaries have been producing new candidates for ordination at about the same rate. Back in

1980 two skilled researchers, Jackson W. Carroll and Robert L. Wilson did a study of the situation. They publicized their report in a book called *Too Many Pastors?* [1] After presenting the empirical data and analyzing the causes, the authors came to their longest chapter, "Survival Tactics for Clergy." In this chapter they set forth eight suggestions as to what could be done in the future to alleviate the problem. Sur-

---

In more cases than not, a new church in the community tends to raise the religious interest of the people in general.

---

prisingly, not a single one of the suggestions was to plant new churches! Apparently the idea never occurred either to the authors or to those they interviewed. If it did, it was rejected as a major opportunity to utilize pastors who had no parish.

Southern Baptists would not allow this to happen. In fact, their Home Mission Board magazine addressed the problem at about the same time saying, "An answer to reaching Southern Baptist Convention goals, and to *employing churchless pastors* seems to be the church planter apprentice program."[2]

The Southern Baptist Church Planter Apprentice program is offered to students in all their seminaries. It is described as "a two-year appointment program for seminary graduates who have limited or no pastoral experience." They offer the young church planters a salary, moving expenses, benefits, and supervision for getting their new church started.

More recently they have developed a new PRAXIS program in which they offer seminary students a 10-week field seminar as part of their degree program with the express purpose of starting a new church in the 10-week period. Southern Baptists believe that seminary students can start new churches because they have observed through the years that it works.

One of my favorite seminaries is the Evangelical Theological Seminary of Indonesia, founded by Chris Marantika. Marantika's goal is to start 50,000 new Indonesian churches using seminary graduates. In order to make this happen, each student must develop a church of at least 30 members to qualify for graduation. In my opinion, that is a final exam worth giving.

WHY PLANT NEW CHURCHES?

There are many reasons for giving church planting a central position in planning strategies for church ministry and mission. By way of summarizing up front much of what will follow in this book, I will list five of the chief reasons:

1. Church planting is biblical. Church planting is the New Testament way of extending the gospel. Trace the expansion of the Church through Jerusalem, Judea, Samaria, and the uttermost part of the earth and you will see that church planters led the way. This is a Kingdom activity, strongly endorsed by God our King. Collectively, as a community of the Kingdom, we can scarcely feel that we are obeying God if we fail to plant churches and plant them intentionally and aggressively.

2. Church planting means denominational survival. While some may not consider institutional survival a worthy motive, deep down in their hearts most church leaders do. Most of us rightly feel that our denominational emphases contribute something important to the wholeness of the universal Body of Christ. But if the present rate of decline in many of the denominations continues for another 25 or 30 years, given the steady rise in the age profile of present membership, the future is bleak to say the least. One of the absolutely essential ingredients for reversing the decline is vigorously planting new churches.

3. *Church planting develops new leadership.* Many studies have confirmed the fact that the most important institutional variable for the growth and expansion of the local church is leadership. In the local church no individual is more important for growth than the senior pastor, but effective senior pastors make it a point to see that lay leaders also take responsible positions in the ministry of the church. For the most part existing churches have unconsciously placed a ·ceiling on both clergy and lay leadership, and as a result upward mobility of new people into positions of ministry is difficult. But new churches open wide the doors of leadership and ministry challenges and the entire Body of Christ subsequently benefits.

4. *Church planting stimulates existing churches.* Some are reluctant to start new churches for fear of harming those churches that are currently located in the target community. They feel that doing so could create undesirable competition between brothers and sisters in Christ. I will develop this in more detail later on, but suffice it to mention here that in more cases than not, a new church in the community tends to raise the religious interest of the people in general and if handled properly can be a benefit to existing churches. That which blesses the kingdom of God as a whole also blesses the churches that truly are a part of the Kingdom.

5. *Church planting is efficient.* There is no more practical or cost effective way of bringing unbelievers to Christ in a given geographical area than planting new churches. This applies both to "new ground" and to "old ground." Let's look at each one.

New Churches on New Ground

By "new ground" I mean areas of the world or people groups within those areas that are as yet unevangelized. As we move into new territory with the gospel, there is little debate that new churches are needed. Yet it is only recently that some very large international evangelistic ministries have begun to realize just how important church planting can be for lasting results.

Three imperatives confirm the need for new churches as an essential part of evangelistic strategy on new ground:

First, there is a *biblical imperative.* As the apostles and evangelists moved out to the unevangelized frontiers they planted new churches. The Apostle Paul said, "It has always been my ambition to preach the gospel where Christ was not known, so that I would not be building on someone else's foundation" (Rom. 15:20). Paul went to new ground, and what did he do? He planted churches.

Second, there is a *demographic imperative.* Of 3 billion people in today's world who do not yet know Jesus Christ as Savior and Lord, around 70 percent do not as yet have a viable, evangelizing church in their culture. This amounts to over 2 billion people. They will not be won to Christ unless someone moves across into their culture with the love of Christ and begins to plant churches. The rapidity at which they are won to Christ will be directly proportional to the rapidity at which churches are multiplied.

Third, there is a *practical imperative.* Some international Christian ministries that have been established for the express purpose of evangelizing have begun to discover that the *most effective evangelistic methodology under heaven is planting new churches.*

Every Home Crusade. The Every Home Crusade (formerly called World Literature Crusade) is a powerful organization that attempts to place Christian literature in every single home in the world. Many individuals and families read the literature and become Christians. As a typical parachurch organization, they at first avoided planting churches because they did not want to be perceived as being in competition with other missions. They wanted to work alongside existing missions.

But Jack McAlister, who served as president of Every Home Crusade for 33 years, was burdened for the thousands of villages in a country like India where no church at all existed. The villages may have been in territories that other missions served, so he did not want to plant churches. Instead he decided to plant "Christ groups." They were fellowships of Christians that functioned something like churches, but for obvious reasons were not called "churches." The results were dramatic. In the state of Andhra Pradesh alone, hundreds of Christ groups have been established. For a time they were planting more than one Christ group per week. In India the organization reports 3,408 Christ groups. The evangelistic effectiveness of Every Home Crusade, in terms of fruit that remains, has been greatly increased.

Youth With A Mission. One of the largest and most energetic of our newer mission agencies is Youth With A Mission (YWAM). Back in 1983 I was invited to do a brief seminar on reaching unreached peoples for YWAM international leadership at their base in Kona, Hawaii. During my personal prayer time that morning, I was strongly impressed by God to tell them to plant new churches. This was not what I had planned at all, but before I began my scheduled teaching, I just told them what I had heard from God that morning. I'll never forget the excitement that swept through that room. It took me several minutes to get them back in order for the agenda of the day.

Several months later I received a letter from Floyd McClung, Jr., YWAM's European Director in Amsterdam, the Netherlands. He was writing on behalf of YWAM leaders from Europe, the Middle East and Africa to affirm that "in that which you shared with us was a directional word for our mission: that is, church planting." The idea of planting churches wasn't entirely new to YWAM; soon afterwards a report was published in *World Christian* stating that YWAM "started, on the average, one church every other day."[3]

"One Million New Churches"

Campus Crusade. Few world class organizations have been used more extensively than Campus Crusade for Christ in evangelistic ministries. However, church planting was not contemplated in their original charter. On college campuses they regularly organized functional substitutes for churches taking the form of campus groups. But the picture became more complex when they developed the *Jesus* film and began direct village evangelism on new ground. There is little question in my mind that worldwide the *Jesus* film is the most powerful evangelistic tool currently in use. Many are saved when it is shown. But Bill Bright began to run into the same problem that Jack McAlister had faced years before. In villages where the *Jesus* film had been shown and numbers of people had prayed to receive Jesus, the believers were not being gathered into Christian churches.

So Campus Crusade began planting "home fellowship groups." It soon became evident that these groups would eventually grow into churches. By necessity, church planting has now become an explicit goal of Campus Crusade. The most massive program they have ever devised is called New Life 2000. In it they are working with Christians from all denominations to achieve eight specific goals by the end of the century. Goal number eight? "Establish in cooperation with existing denominations, more than 1 million new churches." Imagine the impact this is going to have on world evangelization! Look at Thailand as an example. Through the *Jesus* film, Campus Crusade has reported more new churches planted in that country in the 1980s than in the previous 150 years of mission work.

New Churches on Old Ground

With the exception of some evangelistic organizations that excluded church planting when they wrote their charters, most people agree that new churches are necessary for evangelizing people on new ground. But when it comes to the old ground where churches have existed for a hundred or a thousand years, it is a different story. There is much debate on the subject in such traditional bastions of Protestantism as the United States, England, Europe, Canada, Australia, and New Zealand.

In my opinion, the same principle applies to old ground: the most effective evangelistic methodology is planting new churches.

The strongest resistance to the idea comes from the establishment, those individuals whose identity is closely tied in with the traditional churches. I clearly recall the meeting of the Lausanne Committee for World Evangelization held in Pattaya, Thailand in 1980. Over 900 leaders from all over the world were invited to spend 10 days together in strategizing the evangelization of certain significant segments of the world's population. Twenty-three groups met, dealing with the Jews, Chinese, refugees, urban poor, Marxists, Hindus, and many others including "Christian Witness to Nominal Christians Among Protestants." Those who selected this group were largely leaders of traditional churches on old ground.

They deliberated for hours on how to evangelize France, Germany, Australia and many other places, publishing their findings in a 14-page report.[4] I am still appalled that in the report there is not so much as a hint that planting new churches might be a good way to evangelize their areas. I was curious enough to ask around afterwards, and I discovered to my greater consternation that new church planting had been brought up in their deliberations, but they had turned it down as a viable methodology to evangelize their people.

This incident, I think, accurately reflects the attitudes of large numbers of the most influential leaders in traditionally Protestant nations. Little wonder that churches have been declining and Christianity has been losing influence. Their major focus is on the renewal of existing churches. I am one of the strongest supporters of church renewal, and I believe that if renewal comes to our existing churches, much subsequent evangelism will be done. But good as this is, it is not enough. Old wineskins need to be patched, but new wineskins are even more desperately needed.

Remember this simple fact: It's easier to have babies than to raise the dead! Not that all existing churches are dead, or even that most of them are. Most can and should be brought to life by the power of the Holy Spirit. Still the most exciting part of the hospital is the maternity ward.

NOTES

1. Jackson W. Carroll and Robert L. Wilson, *Too Many Pastors? The Clergy Job Market* (New York: The Pilgrim Press, 1980).
2. Janice Trusty, "The Apprentice Approach" (*Missions USA*, January-February, 1983), p. 54.
3. Bryan Bishop, "YWAM Steps Out" (*World Christian*, January-February, 1986), p. 19.
4. "Christian Witness to Nominal Christians Among Protestants," Lausanne Occasional Papers No. 23, 1980.

2

REMOVING THE BARRIERS

The greatest barriers to church planting are in the mind. Once we make up our mind to do it, it can be done. You may have been convinced from the last chapter that there is a direct relationship between church planting and church growth, but is it worth it? Do you believe in church growth at any cost?

This chapter is intended to address such questions as these and others. If you have any personal doubts about church planting, read on. If part of your task is to persuade others that new churches should be planted, read on, for you will certainly face some of the issues I will raise. If you don't have any doubts yourself and if you don't have to convince anyone else, skip the chapter and get on with the how-to part of the book, which is the most important.

THEOLOGICAL REASONS FOR NEW CHURCHES

Those who resist church planting, particularly on old ground, are in most cases trained to think theologically. They are much more open to looking at the pragmatics after they have seen an underlying theological rationale. It is not my intention to develop a systematic theology of church planting here. This has been very well done by David W. Shenk and Ervin R. Stutzman,[1] Charles L. Chaney,[2] Talmadge R. Amberson,[3] and others. But I do want to suggest two theological principles that God has used in the past to change the minds of many skeptics.

The first is the simple, but often elusive fact that each new generation must be evangelized on its own terms. The

---

One of the immediate implications of rapid culture change is that many members of the new generation will not be won to Christ in their parents' churches.

---

basic principle is: *God has no grandchildren.* While parents strongly influence their children toward Jesus Christ, no child is automatically saved just because the parents are. In our modernized Western world, culture change is an accepted fact of life. We no longer live in a society of rural village culture where the expectation was that when the grandchildren grew up their lives and life-styles would be almost identical to those of the grandparents.

One of the immediate implications of rapid culture change is that many members of the new generation will not be won to Christ in their parents' churches.

This became clearer than ever before during the hippie movement that began in the 1960s. Hippies in America formed a true counterculture that was large enough to cause social upheaval. By definition, a counterculture is a deliberate protest against the traditional culture. Therefore, much of what was important to parents became intentionally unimportant to the children. Christian commitment among American hippies was extremely low compared to society as a whole, and very little effective evangelism was being done among hippies during the early years of the movement.

Two facts soon became very clear. For one thing, the hippies didn't like their parents' churches. The churches symbolized social values that were being rejected. For another thing, the existing churches didn't like the hippies. They didn't like the way they looked, the way they dressed, the way they smelled or the way they acted. When a few did find their way into churches they were shunned or, in numerous cases, bodily escorted outside.

Calvary and Vineyard

Quite obviously, the old wineskins were not ready for the new wine. New wineskins were needed, and God brought them into being. He chose some Christian leaders such as Chuck Smith who were humble enough and flexible enough to receive the call to evangelize the hippies. The "Jesus Movement" began, and large numbers of hippies committed their lives to Jesus Christ. Chuck Smith brought them into tents and had them sit on the ground. Beads, Roman sandals, bare feet, shaggy beards, open air nursing of babies, unshampooed hair, and tattered backpacks were quite acceptable in the Sunday service. A new hymnology was quickly developed and adapted to new worship forms. Mass baptisms were held in the Pacific Ocean.

From Chuck Smith's Calvary Chapel movement sprang what is now known as Vineyard Christian Fellowship. Its leader, John Wimber, senses a call to reach the "rock generation," the baby boomers born in the 20-year period following World War II. His vision is to influence the planting of 10,000 churches in America that will be substantially different from traditional churches. Wimber does not want to be different for the sake of being different, but for the sake of reaching a new generation for Christ. And he's doing it.

Not that Calvary Chapel and Vineyard are the only ones reaching baby boomers. My church, Lake Avenue Congregational Church in Pasadena, California, is traditional to the core and yet we are reaching large numbers of baby boomers also. But John Wimber and Chuck Smith are reaching many whom we could not reach. And Rick Warren in Saddleback Valley Community Church, who is their neighbor, is also winning large numbers of baby boomers who would be turned off by Vineyard and Calvary Chapel.

Lost or Wandering Sheep

A second theological issue is that even where there are many sheepfolds, there are still many lost or wandering sheep. God's will for these sheep is clear: *God wants His lost sheep found.* God is "not wanting anyone to perish, but everyone to come to repentance" (2 Pet. 3:9). God's priority is on the lost sheep even more than on those that have been found. Jesus' parable tells us that the shepherd who has 100 sheep and finds only 99 who are safe leaves the 99 and searches for the lost one until it is found (see Luke 15:3-7). Our situation today is not 99 safe and one lost. By the most generous stretch of the imagination we now have more like 30 safe and 70 lost worldwide. We don't have to call in a professional theologian to tell us what this means and where our priorities should be.

Some of the lost or wandering sheep can and will be won into existing churches. But many of them cannot and will not. For them, we need new churches.

A few years ago I went to Germany for the first time and was invited to preach in a Lutheran Church in a medium sized city. I asked how many members the church had and was told there were about 3,000, which was typical of most German Lutheran churches. I was excited about preaching in what sounded like a superchurch until the service started and I saw around 100 in the congregation. They told me that this was slightly above average for a German church.

Naturally, I began thinking of the 2,900. These are lost or wandering sheep. God wants them found and brought into the sheepfold. If the church I preached in experienced a revival in which people were filled with the Holy Spirit, I have no doubt that many of them would get more involved in that same church. But I am equally sure that not all of them would. Many of them have decided that they don't like that old church no matter what happens, but they could be open to new churches with philosophies of ministry geared more directly to their generational culture and their felt needs.

SIX EMPIRICAL REASONS FOR NEW CHURCHES

Many barriers to church planting begin to crumble when the practical benefits are understood. Christian leaders are usually more pragmatic than they are inclined to admit. Deep down they are impressed if something works. Here are six ways in which new churches work.

1. *New churches are a key to outreach.* I have affirmed time and again that planting new churches enhances evangelism. Much research has been done to confirm this, but the insights gained have not readily been applied to denominational programming.

I was privileged to participate in a consortium sponsored by the mainline denominations over the three years 1976 through 1978. They had then been declining for over 10 years and were beginning to become concerned enough to ask why. When the report was published, Lyle Schaller, who is highly regarded as perhaps the most knowledgeable person in America about church dynamics, wrote this: "Every denomination reporting an increase in membership reports an increase in the number of congregations. Every denomination reporting an increase in the total number of congregations reports an increase in members. Every denomination reporting a decrease in membership reports a decrease in congregations. Every denomination reporting a decrease in congregations reports a decrease in members."[4]

This is a highly significant finding. Schaller, who is trying to help the traditional churches break out of their doldrums and reverse their growth curves, tells them that in order to do so they must remove the barrier of neglecting church planting. He says, "The first step in developing a denominational strategy for church growth should be to organize new congregations."[5]

2. New churches grow better than old churches. Built into new churches is a potential for growth that older churches no longer have. This does not mean that older churches cannot grow. They often do. Nor does it mean that all new churches grow. Frequently they do not. But across the board, growth is more likely with less effort in newer churches.

Phil Jones, a researcher for the Southern Baptist Home Mission Board, reports: "If baptism rates per 100 members are used as a measure of efficiency for a church, then young churches are more efficient than old churches. The older a church gets, the less efficient it is in baptizing new converts."[6]

The late Keith Lusk did a similar study of churches of all denominations in the Santa Clarita Valley of California and found that in 1986 older churches were baptizing at the rate of four baptisms per 100 members per year, while newer churches were baptizing at the rate of 16 baptisms per 100 members. It is not surprising, then, that over all growth increases as new churches are started.

My friend, Carl F. George, director of the Charles E. Fuller Institute of Evangelism and Church Growth in

---

Church leaders who think that geographical location is more important than social networks to the average unchurched American are living far from reality.

Pasadena, California, was called in for consultation with the leaders of a regional body of one of the mainline denominations. They wanted him to identify barriers to growth. He discovered a budget item of $250,000 per year for the support of a number of "missions" that in 30 years had not been able to become viable enough to support themselves. He also discovered that they said they couldn't afford to plant new churches. George wisely persuaded them to close the missions and divert the $250,000 per year into new church development. It made all the difference in the world.

3. *New churches provide more options for the unchurched.* Unbelievers come in such a wide variety that a correspondingly wide variety of church options is needed to win them. Fortunately, no two churches are just alike and new churches are different from others even in their same denomination.

Some church planners have an aversion to starting churches of the same denomination in geographical proximity to each other. This may be wise in rural or small town settings, but it makes little sense in most of today's urban areas. In the same neighborhood one often finds a considerable variety of ethnic groups, social classes, and other social networks, each of which require a different kind of church. Church leaders who think that geographical location is more important than social networks to the average unchurched American are living far from reality.

4. *New churches are usually needed.* One common barrier to new church planting is the notion that "this area is already overchurched." Most such evaluations are off target.

Yes, I will admit that some areas might be *adequately* churched. Take Prinsburg, Minnesota, for example. Just a few years ago the Christian Reformed Church there had 850 members with average attendance of 700 each Sunday. The town itself counted only 557 people! Adequately churched? I thought so until I learned that in 1984 the church council there decided that it might be desirable to start a second church in town. The reasons given were varied: the church was already full, the abilities and gifts of many members were not being used, a new church could provide closer fellowship, and the beginning of a new church might provide a greater emphasis on evangelism.

About 130 members left the mother church in 1984 and started a new church just a couple blocks away. Today there are approximately 200 members in the new church with 140 to 150 in attendance every Sunday. A high percentage of the members have become involved in evangelistic outreach of one kind or another and the church has developed a widely recognized and effective jail ministry.

Many in the mother church who previously were but little involved in church activities have actively assumed positions of leadership. Prinsburg, I would say, is far better off than it was.

It may be possible for a rural area to be adequately churched, but I doubt if a single urban area in the United States is adequately churched. Demographic studies of urban areas invariably reveal rather astounding numbers of unchurched, desperately in need of new churches if they are going to be reached for Christ. One of the reasons the Church of God in Christ is among America's fastest growing denominations is that they encourage the multiplication of urban storefront churches even on successive blocks in the inner city.

5. New churches help denominations survive. Churches, like people, die. Just to stay even without showing any growth at all, denominations need to replace their deceased churches. This makes it necessary to start at least some new churches each year unless leaders are indifferent to their own denomination's viability.

One of the reasons the Presbyterian Church (U.S.A.) has been declining is that its northern segment decreased their church planting efforts from 77 per year in the 1950s to 25 per year in the 1960s and to 18 per year in the 1970s They lost some 50,000 members each year between 1964 and 1974. During that same period of time, however, the new churches that they did start were serving 50,000 Presbyterians and contributed $3.25 million to the national denominational office. If twice as many churches had been started, the picture would have been quite different.

6. New churches help meet the needs of existing Christians. Up to now virtually all my emphasis on planting new churches has been focused on reaching unchurched. This is certainly the highest priority motivation for new churches. Nevertheless, a secondary function of helping many who are already Christians and church members should not be ignored.

The ways that new people come into the church are biological growth (the children of members), transfer growth (Christians who move from one church to another), and conversion growth (new Christians joining a church for the first time). Conversion growth represents the most dynamic expansion of the Kindgom, and might be considered the most important form of church growth. However, we should not shy away from transfer growth. Why?

The most obvious reason is that we live in a mobile society and when new Christian people move into our neighborhood the polite thing to do is to invite them to attend and become members of our church. Of course other churches will be doing the same with them, and in this day and age it is most likely that they will decide not necessarily on the church of their former denomination, but on the church that they perceive can best meet their personal and family needs. If our church attracts them it is because we are doing something of high value to them and the growth they bring is good growth.

But there is another reason. In almost any given community there are some Christians who have not been growing in their spiritual lives and who are not particularly contributing to the kingdom of God simply because they do not fit into their present church situation. What they really need is to change churches and join one in which they fit.

This is difficult for many of us to admit, especially when our church is the one not meeting their needs. Our tendency is to put the blame on them rather than on the church. But I am not sure that there should be blame on either side. After all, there is nothing eternal about local church membership. No church that I have joined has asked me to pledge "until death do us part." The reason is that we know theologically that the local church should not be regarded as an end in itself. The kingdom of God is the end and local churches are simply instruments of the Kingdom. Some, unfortunately, have become dull instruments and to that degree they have disqualified themselves for kingdom service. Others are not particularly dull instruments, but they are operating under a philosophy of ministry that could not be expected to meet the needs of certain people.

When it comes down to choosing between people's needs or our institution's needs, clearly the people should take the priority. We should affirm what is best for them. In numerous cases new churches in the community have provided just what many people needed.

If you are among those who actively advocate church planting, particularly if you are engaged in persuading others, you can anticipate receiving one or more of the standard objections to church planting. I will list the objections I have heard the most under the categories of pragmatic objections and ethical objections.

PRAGMATIC OBJECTIONS TO CHURCH PLANTING

If your plan is for a given local church to take the initiative in sending off members to start a new church, some will likely express their fear that it may harm the parent church.

In reality, with proper planning, the reverse is more likely. It will usually help the present church. Underlying this is the application of the biblical promise, "Give, and it will be given to you. A good measure, pressed down, shaken together and running over" (Luke 6:38). We mostly apply this to giving money, but I believe it applies just as well to a church willing to give some of its people for the advancement of God's kingdom.

I watched God do this some years ago when my church, Lake Avenue Congregational Church, sent off 60 members one Sunday morning to start the Sunrise Community Church in a nearby city. We had mixed feelings because as of the following Sunday we knew we would no longer see our brothers and sisters whom we loved very much. But that evening purely by coincidence we also had scheduled a reception of new members. God gave us 65 of them! We felt that He had kept His promise on the same day.

Brian Larson's doctoral studies at Talbot Theological Seminary show that ordinarily the parent church that spins off members to start a new church finds them replaced in six months. The same holds true for finances. But he also discovered that the pattern depends to a significant degree on the attitude of the parent church, particularly the pastor. If the pastor has a negative attitude toward the church planting process it might negatively affect the parent church's subsequent growth.[7]

The Start-up Cost

A second pragmatic objection you will hear is that we can't plant new churches because the start-up cost is too high.

The truth of the matter is that in terms of dollars spent by the sponsoring church or agency, new church planting can be the most cost effective method of evangelization.

I like Lyle Schaller's reply to some Methodist leaders who told him that if they started 500 new churches they would need $100 million, and that there was no way they could find the money. Schaller says, "That is the wrong question based on questionable assumptions....A better beginning point is the Great Commission (Matt. 28:18-20)."[8] I wish denominational executives across the board would listen to what he is saying and act on it.

Back in 1980 I was invited to do a pastors' seminar for a presbytery in Texas. They were rather pleased to tell me that they had started two new churches in the past decade and that they were planning another for the 1980s I asked them why only one. "That's all we can afford right now," they replied. On impulse I asked them how much each one cost and they told me it was $500,000 per church. I made a mental note.

One month later I did a similar seminar for the pastors of an Assemblies of God district in North Carolina. The district was about the same size as the presbytery. As I was having lunch with the district superintendent, Charles Cookman, I asked him how many new churches they had started in the 1970s "Oh," he said, "I'm glad you asked. We set a goal of 70 new churches for the seventies, but we actually planted 85." Again on impulse I asked him how much they cost. He did some calculations on his paper place mat and said, "Each one cost about $2,500."

No wonder the growth rate of the Assemblies of God is several times that of the Presbyterian Church (U.S.A.). It costs Presbyterians 200 times as much to start a new church!

Of course, the Presbyterians operate on a set of assumptions that the Assemblies of God do not. They assume that the founding pastor needs a college and seminary education, that he or she needs to be paid a full salary on par with pastors of established churches, and that land and a building are necessary up front. Those assumptions require a substantial budget. In the long run the Assemblies of God church is also worth $500,000, but their assumption is that the money to pay for staff, land, and buildings should come from the people subsequently won into the new church rather than up front.

A final pragmatic objection frequently heard is that sending off people to start a new church will break longstanding Christian fellowship.

I have no answer for this except to say that it is true, and it is one of the prices that must be paid for new churches. But I would point out that if the average member of the objecting church receives a promotion and raise in salary that requires a job transfer, few will complain that longstanding Christian fellowship will be broken. In the big picture, winning the lost to Jesus Christ might be a higher value than preserving fellowship, sweet as it may be.

ETHICAL OBJECTIONS

Ethically-oriented objections to planting new churches generally focus on two issues: love and unity.

Some fear that if we move into a community where churches are already located, our new church may harm the others. Christian love tells us to help other churches, not harm them.

Studies have shown that when a new church moves into an area, a force field frequently develops that in fact can help the churches already there. The whole religious consciousness of the community can rise. My friend, Glenn Akers, did a study of the town of Ewa on Hawaii's Oahu Island when he planted a Southern Baptist church there a few years ago. He found that the attendance in the Roman Catholic Church rose by 100 percent, the Congregational Church attendance rose by 155 percent, and even the two Buddhist temples each showed a 33 percent increase in attendance.

I believe it is important and beneficial to enjoy the approval of existing churches when a new church is planted. But while such approval is a plus, it should not be regarded as a prerequisite. As the parable of the shepherd indicates, the needs of the lost are a higher consideration than the needs of those who are safe and sound in the churches. As we learn from the modern shopping mall theory of merchandising, two churches even in close proximity to each other will reach many more unchurched than either one could hope to do alone.

The Question of Unity

But how about the ethics of church planting? The doctrine of Christian unity says we should be getting together rather than proliferating and confusing the public with so many differing and at times competing forms of Christianity.

This would be a valid position if the existing churches were doing an adequate job of reaching and winning the unchurched in the community. But such is rarely the case. Most communities have a large unreaped harvest of unbelievers, and Jesus tells us to pray that the Lord will send more, not fewer, laborers into the harvest field (see Matt. 9:37-38).

Of course, many pastors of existing churches harbor an underlying fear that if a new church comes to their community some of their members might choose to transfer their membership there. The subsequent accusation of "sheep stealing" is not uncommon. But Donald McGavran, the father of the church growth movement, has frequently said, "Well fed sheep cannot be stolen." "Sheep stealing" is usually a cry of agony from a non-growing church. Pastors of growing churches typically take a far different position. In fact, if they have members who are not developing spiritually and who are discontent for any reason, they will eagerly help them transfer to a new church and give them their blessing. Both churches are frequently better off for the change.

Look closely at Jesus' prayer for unity in John 17. His prayer for unity is quite task-oriented. "That all of them may be one,...that the world may believe that You sent Me" (John 17:21, *NKJV*). It seems that Jesus is saying that any form of Christian unity that helps evangelization is desirable. On the other hand, unity that raises a barrier to evangelization may be true unity, but it is not what Jesus was praying for.

Appeals to Christian love and Christian unity should be geared toward encouraging church planting and thereby contribute to evangelizing the unchurched.

NOTES

1. David W. Shenk and Ervin R. Stutzman, *Creating Communities of the Kingdom: New Testament Models of Church Planting* (Scottdale, PA: Herald Press, 1988). See chapter 1, "The Church and Its Message."

2. Charles L. Chaney, *Church Planting at the End of the Twentieth Century* (Wheaton, IL: Tyndale House, 1982). See chapter 1, "Biblical Pillars for Church Planting."

3. Talmadge R. Amberson, *The Birth of Churches: A Biblical Basis for Church Planting* (Nashville, TN: Broadman Press, 1979). See especially chapter 1, "The Foundation for Church Planting" by Talmadge R. Amberson and chapter 9, "The Holy Spirit and the Birth of Churches," by J. Terry Young.

4. Lyle E. Schaller, "Commentary: What Are the Alternatives?" *Understanding Church Growth and Decline 1950-1978* (New York, NY: The Pilgrim Press, 1979), p. 351.

5. Ibid.

6. Phil Jones, "An Examination of the Statistical Growth of the Southern Baptist Convention" *Understanding Church Growth and Decline 1950-1978* (New York, NY: The Pilgrim Press, 1979), p. 170.

7. Brian L. Larson, *Church Planting Mother-Daughter Style: A Study of Procedures and Results*, D.Min. dissertation. Talbot Theological Seminary, La Mirada, CA, 1984.

8. Lyle E. Schaller, "Why Start New Churches?" (*The Circuit Rider*, May, 1979), p. 80.

3

ESSENTIALS FOR PLANNING

I am by nature an activist. When I have a job to do, I want to move out and begin getting the job done. But through the years I have discovered time and again that the best way to get any job done and done properly is to spend time up front planning. I fully realize that planning can be overemphasized; some of my friends, I'm afraid, seem to spend all their time planning and they very seldom get around to doing. Planning can become an end in itself, but there is a balance, a happy medium, where an appropriate amount of previous planning multiplies efficiency when the actual work begins.

One of my friend Robert Schuller's modern day proverbs goes: *If you fail to plan, you're planning to fail.* Think about this, and you will agree that it's as true as can be. All too many of us find ourselves described variously as chasing rabbits, spinning our wheels, shadow boxing, wasting our time, or reinventing the wheel—principally because we did not plan or did so poorly. Planning takes time. It takes mental energy. It takes patience. At times it takes using the eraser more than the pencil. But doing it is more than worth the cost.

As you begin the process of planting a new church, my best initial advice for you is to start planning to plan. Long before Robert Schuller, Solomon knew this when he said, "The wise man looks ahead. The fool attempts to fool himself and won't face facts" (Prov. 14:8, *TLB*).

How do you plan for starting a new church? I believe there are two highly important aspects involved: the spiritual aspect and the technical aspect. Let's look at them one at a time.

THE SPIRITUAL ASPECT

Not too long ago, I am embarrassed to say, it would have been quite difficult to find a church growth book that placed the spiritual aspect of planning front and center in more than a token way. No longer, however. It was back in the late '70s when good friends like Professor Herbert Kane of Trinity Evangelical Divinity School began getting on our case. Kane evaluated the Church Growth Movement as "the most dynamic movement in mission circles in recent years," but went on to say that "The proponents of church growth, with few exceptions, have emphasized the human factors and all but overlooked the divine factor."[1] We recognized that there was much truth in what they were saying, so many of us began to look seriously into the working of the Holy Spirit in church growth.

My own pilgrimage, first of all, took me on a seven-year project of researching the relationship between supernatural signs and wonders and the growth of churches worldwide. Not only did I discover that God was using supernatural signs and wonders in the spread of the gospel today much as He did in the book of Acts, but in the process I myself became a practitioner and have seen God do some miraculous things through me and through many with whom I associate.

Then another problem arose. Some of the same friends who were concerned that I had not dealt with the spiritual aspect of church growth enough became fearful that I had "gone charismatic." In an attempt to help them understand

---

The more deeply I dig beneath the surface of church growth principles, the more thoroughly convinced I become that the real battle is a spiritual battle and that our principal weapon is prayer.

---

that I was still nothing but an evangelical Congregationalist, I coined the term "Third Wave," which has since caught on. If the first wave of the modern outpouring of the Holy Spirit was the Pentecostal movement and the second wave was the charismatic movement, the Third Wave is also spreading among evangelicals who differ from the first two waves in some secondary matters, but see the miraculous power of the Holy Spirit moving through them in much the same way.[2]

Planning for a healing ministry may or may not be appropriate as you consider planting a new church. Timing is crucial, and for some this kind of an innovation may not as yet fit. But a second spiritual aspect that quite certainly can be more universally and immediately applied, is prayer.

Prayer

The more deeply I dig beneath the surface of church growth principles, the more thoroughly convinced I become that the real battle is a spiritual battle and that our principal weapon is prayer.

Over the three or four decades of the history of the Church Growth Movement some excellent technology has been developed. Donald McGavran's seminal insights have been broadened, refined, experimented with, applied in numerous cultures and praised by many Christian leaders who have found that they work. I myself have joined him and many others in research, analysis, consultation, training, and programming. Most of the balance of this book is given to explaining how you can use basic church growth principles to plant a new church. I want to be among the first to applaud the practical, technical aspects of church growth.

But I also want to be among the first to affirm as strongly as possible that all the technology, good as it may be, will never be utilized to its maximum potential in planting churches unless and until the spiritual battle is engaged and won. We can move forward by hobbling along, but it is better to run. An automobile can operate on four or five cylinders, but it is better if all eight are firing.

Many of our technical church growth principles could be used to grow fast food restaurants or insurance companies or tire stores. These can succeed without prayer because they are human institutions. Churches cannot. Jesus said, "I will build my church" (Matt. 16:18), and He is the only one who ultimately does it. We are instruments in His hands for the task, and therefore we must be in tune with what He is doing and how He wants it done if we hope to be useful and effective instruments. Knowing what God is doing is a spiritual activity. If the church we plant is not a divine institution, it is not the kind of church we want.

We would be naive to ignore the fact that Satan desires just the opposite. He would like to see no church planted at all. But he would be equally happy if the church that is planted turns out to be a carnal church where the works of the flesh are more prominent than the fruit of the Spirit. Satan sees every new church as an invasion of his kingdom, and he will use every possible tactic to stop or neutralize our efforts. The Bible alerts us to this and sensitizes us to the wiles of the devil. It also tells us that the weapons of our warfare are spiritual, not carnal (see 2 Cor. 10:4).

The American Christian public has never been as aware as it is now of both the wiles of the devil and the power of prayer. Chief stimulants of this awareness have been Frank Peretti's novels starting with *This Present Darkness*.[3] The most prominent theme running through these books is that the prayers of ordinary Christian people can have a crucial influence in weakening the forces of evil and strengthening the forces of good. I am convinced that this has a direct application to planting new churches.

Planning a Prayer Ministry

How, then, should we plan our prayer ministry as we move out to plant a church? I believe there are four things we need to consider very seriously:

1. *The leaders themselves should improve their own prayer life.* All the leaders of the church planting effort, but particularly the church planter or the founding pastor should take conscious and deliberate steps to be sure their prayer life is up to par. What this will mean for one may not be the same as what it will mean for another. For most, however, it will begin with increasing the amount of time per day specifically set aside to pray.

Research indicates that the average American pastor spends from 15 to 22 minutes per day in prayer. One in four spends less than 10 minutes. Pastors with whom I have discussed this almost universally admit that they do not pray as much as they really think they should even at their own minimum standards.

Much of this can be corrected by a mere act of will. The best way to start praying longer is to decide to do it. One of the most helpful guides for this is Larry Lea's book, *Could You Not Tarry One Hour?* [4] I believe that Lea is realistic in challenging us to work on expanding our personal prayer time to one hour per day. Every Christian leader I know could do it if they decided to. I have lived too long to buy into the excuse that "my schedule won't permit it."

One of the most positive suggestions that Larry Lea has for activists like me is to use the Lord's Prayer daily as a framework for the entire prayer time. Since many church planters are also activists, I recommend that they consider doing this. Some will follow Larry Lea's outline in more detail than others, but the general framework can apply to all.

2. Develop the habit of group or corporate prayer. Those whom God has called to start the new church should set aside significant time to pray together on a regular basis, even if the number is as small as one or two families. As group prayer is added to personal prayer, spiritual power increases proportionately.

If group prayer starts in the planning stage, the habit will more than likely continue through the nucleus building phase and into the life of the new church. Keep in mind that the dynamics of group prayer begin to diminish when the group grows to over 17 persons. At 20 or so the shift should be made from group prayer to corporate prayer. This is not an appropriate place to detail the differences between the two, but suffice it to say that while group prayer is participant intensive, corporate prayer is leader intensive. The group prayer can flow to a large extent by itself. Corporate

prayer, particularly as it grows larger, requires skilled leadership, but not leadership that dominates and overshadows
the immediate direction of the Holy Spirit.

**3. *Enlist personal intercessors for the church
planter and other leaders.*** Intercession for Christian
leaders is perhaps the most underutilized source of spiritual
power in our churches today. A major cause of this is igno-
rance, pure and simple. Very few Christian leaders I speak
to have given serious thought to enlisting personal intercessors, and I am persuaded that this is one of the causes of
the unusual epidemic of falling Christian leaders we are
seeing in these days.

In most churches or circles of Christian acquaintance, I
believe that God has already called specific men and
women, some of whom may have the spiritual gift of intercession and some of whom may not, to pray for their pastors and other leaders. My friend, John Maxwell, pastor of
Skyline Wesleyan Church in San Diego, California, has
enlisted a committed group of 100 men who intercede for
him on a daily basis. Another friend, Mike Flynn, rector of
St. Jude's Episcopal Church in Burbank, California, heard
about this for the first time, spent six months in enlisting
and encouraging 18 prayer partners, and testifies to a measurably more powerful ministry ever since. He also claims
much less attack in the areas of temptation, accusation, and
harassment and attributes this to his intercessors doing battle for him in prayer.

I myself have 17 prayer partners who have come to play
an essential role in my ministry. One of the 17 is what I call
an I-1 intercessor, with whom I maintain close contact. The
other 16 are I-2 intercessors, with whom I maintain a regular but somewhat casual contact. Six of them have the gift
of intercession, while the other 11 are simply good Christian people who have felt a call of God to pray for my wife,

Doris, and myself on a daily basis. Added to this I have a number of I-3 intercessors with whom I have a quite remote contact, but who also pray for me regularly.

If it is true that the real battle in church planting is a spiritual battle, I cannot recommend enlisting personal intercessors too highly.

4. Be aware of spiritual warfare. As I analyze the dynamics of personal intercession, particularly in the light of Ephesians 6:10-22, I have concluded that personal intercession is so effective because it is a form of spiritual warfare. We wrestle not against flesh and blood, but against principalities and powers. We need the full armor of God, activated by the Holy Spirit, praying always with all prayer and supplication in the Spirit.

It is becoming clearer that spiritual warfare takes place on at least two levels: the level of personal deliverance and wrestling with principalities and powers. Satan attacks individuals with the world, the flesh, and the devil (demonic forces). He aims his bow and arrow especially at leaders, and especially at leaders who are planting churches. Through prayer, these attacks can be neutralized and the gospel can spread.

On the higher level there may well be ranking demonic spirits assigned to territories or nations or neighborhoods or cities or affinity groups that need to be dealt with. Only a little is known about these territorial spirits and about this type of spiritual warfare, but particularly since the appearance of *This Present Darkness,* interest in learning more about them is rapidly increasing.

I realize that some of our church traditions are not especially tuned in to spiritual warfare on either level, and I am not suggesting that this is a requirement for successful church planting across the board. But I do think that in this day and age it is at least prominent enough to mention in a book of this nature. As we plan to plant a church we should be aware that some of Satan's attacks might be aimed directly at us, and that God has equipped us with the necessary power through the cross of Christ to overcome them.

THE TECHNICAL ASPECT

If the spiritual bases are covered, planning for the new church should go on to include four very important elements: a church planter, some church people, a philosophy of ministry, and research.

A Church Planter

As I will reiterate time and again, the leader is the principal key to a successful church planting endeavor. There are many other important components of church planting, but they will stand or fall depending on the leadership available. I have analyzed church leadership in general in my book *Leading Your Church to Growth*,[5] and of all my books, that is the one I would recommend the most as a companion to this one.

The characteristics of an ideal church planter are not the same as those of the pastor of an existing church, although there is considerable overlap. Characteristics of church planters themselves will differ according to two important variables: (1) Whether the church planter intends to be the founding pastor; and (2) Whether the projected size of the church is over 200 or under 200. As we will see, planning for the new church can go either way in either category. However, assuming for the moment that the church planter is a founding pastor and that the projected size of the new church is over 200, here is a profile of the church planter:

1. *A committed Christian worker.* Church planters need to be people of God. They need to be sure of their salvation through Jesus Christ. They need to know what it means to trust God when things are going well and when they are not. They need to be people of prayer, as I have explained previously. Loving God and serving Him need to be their top priorities of life.

2. *A self-starter.* Church planters are their own boss. They do not punch a time clock and follow someone else's orders. Because they arrange their own schedules their daily productivity depends on their personal ability to get up in the morning, scope out a day's work, and hang in there until the task is completed. This requires self-discipline. It requires time management skills. For many the temptation to sleep in, pursue hobbies, watch television, multiply social engagements, or putter around the house is too much to resist, and consequently the new church suffers.

3. *Willing to endure loneliness.* Pastors of existing churches for the most part come to depend on the loving strokes they receive from their people for their emotional well being. This is good, and it will eventually develop in the new church. But it is not common at first. Starting a new church is frequently a lonely job, full of frustrations. This is why church planters need to be people who are not easily discouraged. They need to apply possibility thinking, as Robert Schuller would say. They need to take setbacks in stride, like a football running back, knowing that touchdowns usually come only after getting knocked down many, many times.

4. *Adaptable.* Flexibility is very important for church planters. This is one reason, as I mentioned in a previous chapter, that new seminary or Bible school graduates are excellent candidates to plant new churches. For many the first few years of professional ministry are the most flexible.

Later on, rigidity sets in. The family comes along, children get into school, house and car payments become necessities of life, and moving around is not easy at all. But young people right out of seminary typically are prepared to serve God in almost any way He indicates. They, like the apostle Paul, are willing to be abased and willing to abound. These qualities go a long way in contributing to a successful new church start.

Other Vital Qualities...Including Faith

5. *A high level of faith.* Church planters not only need to believe in God, they also need to believe in themselves. That is, they need to be convinced that God can and will do great things through them. They need to be people of healthy self-esteem. The recognition that they are chosen instruments of God for a significant task in the kingdom is not a sign of pride, but of humility, a humble willingness to be a servant of the Most High.

In developing the aggressive church planting program for Liberty Baptist Fellowship in conjunction with Jerry Falwell's Liberty Baptist Seminary, Elmer Towns observed the vital role of faith in church planting. He thoroughly researched the role that faith played in the lives and ministries of ten successful Baptist church planters and reports those findings in *Stepping Out on Faith*. He found that "Whether the pastor believes that faith is causal/interventional, or faith is passive/instrumental....those pastors with the strongest perception of their faith also have growing churches."[6]

6. *Supportive spouse and family.* From time to time my students will come to me and say, "I'm taking your course and through it God is calling me to plant a new church when I get out of seminary. But I have talked it over with my wife, and she does not feel led in that direction at all. What should I do?"

My response is that I have ordered my life around what I believe to be three biblical priorities: commitment to Christ; commitment to the Body of Christ, and commitment to the work of Christ in the world. They are all essential, but the order can't be changed. Commitment to the Body of Christ includes both the nuclear family and the spiritual family. Therefore I never recommend leading a new church start (the work of Christ in the world) unless the spouse is in full support. I also counsel my students to pray sincerely that God will change the attitude of a reluctant spouse. Human coercion rarely works well. A person convinced against their will is of the same opinion still. But through prayer, God can change the will and the couple can move out in harmony to plant the church.

7. *Willing and able to lead.* Leadership is crucial. It is too bad that this turns out to be one of the weakest areas in pastoral ministry. Seminaries typically do not teach students how to lead. They learn how to perform the prescribed religious duties well. They learn a bit about how to administer or manage a church, usually assuming a maintenance mode, not a growth mode. Few, however, learn to lead a church for growth. Despite this, some seminary graduates have excellent leadership abilities and these are the ones who will usually make the best church planters. I agree with John Maxwell that everything rises or falls on leadership.

8. *A friendly personality.* Some individuals have a quality about them that makes strangers like them and trust them almost immediately. Some have the ability to relate well to the unchurched and not to feel intimidated by non-Christians or uncomfortable in close contact with a worldly life-style. These characteristics are particularly useful in starting a new church. They are, of course, valuable in existing churches as well, but they are not as essential there as in church planting.

9. *Clearly called by God to plant a church.* I purposely began this profile with commitment to God and end it with the call of God. All the other characteristics are sandwiched in between. Moving out to start a new church is no

---

Even if your goal is to reach the unchurched, it is good to have people around you who have had some experience in what a church is and how it usually functions.

Sunday School picnic. It is a difficult, strenuous, frustrating and demanding task. I do not recommend that anyone undertake this ministry without being sure that they are in the will of God. Nothing could be more disastrous than getting way down the road in new church development and waking up one morning only to discover that God has not been there. The best way to avoid this is to make specific plans for suggested prayer as I suggested earlier in the chapter.

These nine characteristics of a church planter are not exhaustive. Others with more skill than I in career counselling have developed even more sophisticated models.[7] Furthermore they are simply a profile. By that I mean that if a church planter candidate does not score high on all nine, it does not necessarily mean they are disqualified from planting a church. Nevertheless, the general profile should be higher than average if the prospects for success are going to be reasonably good.

Some Church People

When planning for a new church, plan to have some church people in the nucleus. Even if your goal is to reach the unchurched, it is good to have people around you who have had some experience in what a church is and how it usually functions.

I am aware that some recommend that when we start a new church by using telemarketing or other means it is best to start with a group of unchurched people and develop them into a church. I can understand where they are coming from. They say that if we want new wineskins to contain the new wine, we do not need those who are dragging old wineskins around with them to get in the way. And this has worked in some instances. It is my opinion, however, that most church planters would do well to have a core of people around them who bring some of the technical skills that unchurched people would not have.

If the new church starts with a nucleus that breaks off from an existing church, naturally church people will be there. If not, another source is locating those who were once church members but who currently are not attending a church. National surveys show that about 15 million Americans consider themselves born-again Christians and believe the whole Bible, but do not attend church. The surveys also show that the number one reason why they are not currently in a church is that they haven't been invited, and there is no reason why you can't invite them.

A further, more risky, source of church people for the new church is those who are dissatisfied with their present church affiliation and who are looking for another option. The risk is that among them might be some chronic complainers whom you do not especially need, but more than likely they will be good-hearted Christians who feel that God is opening up new avenues for Christian growth and service.

A Philosophy of Ministry

In the earliest stages of planning it is good to have a fairly clear idea as to what kind of a church you feel God is leading you to plant. The description of this is called a philosophy of ministry. While you will need to keep working on and revising your philosophy of ministry as you move down the road of church planting, the more basic work you can do on it up front the better.

The philosophy of ministry, which I will explain in more detail later, answers two fundamental questions: Who? and How? *Who* is God calling us and equipping us to reach? And *how* are we going to do it?

Clear answers to these questions at the beginning will help avoid two potential pitfalls. (1) If all new members of the nucleus and then the church read and understand the philosophy of ministry from day one, dissentions and misunderstandings down the line will be avoided. (2) If the target audience is clearly understood and described, there will be much less danger of wasteful and inefficient efforts to penetrate unresponsive populations. These two reasons alone make it clear that you do not plan well for a new church start unless you invest the time and energy necessary to articulate your philosophy of ministry.

Research

Along with the church planter, church people, and a philosophy of ministry, the fourth ingredient for the planning stage is research. Appropriate research will help you to know your target audience well and select a site for the new church that best fits your purpose. I will detail how this research is done in a later chapter, but meanwhile let's keep in mind that it must be done. As the Bible says, "What a shame—yes, how stupid!—to decide before knowing the facts!" (Prov. 18:13, *TLB*). Research will help us know the relevant facts, make intelligent decisions, and see that the new church gets the best start possible.

NOTES
1. J. Herbert Kane, *The Christian World Mission Today and Tomorrow* (Grand Rapids, MI: Baker Book House, 1981), pp. 201, 212.
2. I summarize all of this and my other findings in my book *How to Have a Healing Ministry Without Making Your Church Sick* (Ventura, CA: Regal Books, 1988).
3. Frank Peretti, *This Present Darkness*, (Westchester, IL: Crossway Books, 1986).
4. Larry Lea, *Could You Not Tarry One Hour?* (Lake Mary, FL: Creation House, 1987).
5. C. Peter Wagner, *Leading Your Church to Growth* (Ventura, CA: Regal Books, 1984).
6. Jerry Falwell and Elmer Towns, *Stepping Out in Faith* (Wheaton, IL: Tyndale House Publishers, 1984), p. 165.
7. For a professionally developed tool to identify potential church planters, see Charles R. Ridley, *How to Select Church Planters: A Self-Study Manual for Recruiting, Screening, Interviewing, and Evaluating Qualified Church Planters* (Pasadena, CA: Fuller Evangelistic Association, 1988).

4

TWELVE GOOD WAYS TO PLANT A CHURCH

There are many ways to plant a church, quite probably more than 12. I have selected these 12, however, because they all work. I'm sure that they won't all work for you, but I am equally sure that one or more of them will. Each church planting endeavor carries its own set of circumstances that will help determine which method is best.

My students often ask me which of the 12 methods I recommend the most highly. But I cannot answer that question in a general way. I could only answer it on a case-by-case basis. That's why I call them "12 good ways." I agree with what Rick Warren of Saddleback Valley Community Church in Mission Viejo, California, says: "If you're getting the job done, I like the way you're doing it."

While I list the methods with numbers one through twelve, they fall naturally into two general categories for which I am going to use some technical church growth terminology: *modality models* and *sodality models*. I realize that these are strange words to some, but I'm using them because I have not been able to find any nontechnical synonyms with which I am comfortable. Generally, "modality" refers to congregational structures; "sodality" refers to other structures, such as denominational or parachurch agencies, which are not based in the local congregation.

MODALITY MODELS

The modality models for church planting all involve one local church giving birth to another. Seven of the 12 methods fall into the modality category.

Using the local church as a base has several built-in advantages for the new church, particularly when the nucleus for the new church is formed by people from the parent congregation itself. For one thing, the nucleus will contain church people with some experienced Christian lay leaders. For another, the nucleus members are usually characterized by a higher than average commitment level. When a pastor challenges members of an existing congregation to move out and start a new church for the glory of God, usually the more committed are the first to respond. A final advantage is that the nucleus members come to the project with a general agreement on philosophy of ministry. Not that the new church should be a clone, but the fundamental assumptions will usually be in place.

The first four methods of planting churches all assume that the parent church will spawn daughter congregations with the specific intent that the offspring will end up as autonomous churches. This is not the only possible outcome of modality models, as we will see, but it is characteristic of these first four.

1. *Hiving off*. Hiving off is the most common way of planting a daughter church. It simply means that the members of a local congregation are challenged to form a nucleus and at a predetermined time, these people will move out under the leadership of a church planter and become the charter members of a new congregation. This usually assumes that the new church will be in the same general geographical area so that the nucleus members will not be expected to make a residential move.

Frequently the selection of the nucleus members is random. All those who feel the call of God and who are willing to accept the challenge are welcome to apply. At other

---

Using the local church as a base has several built-in advantages for the new church, particularly when the nucleus for the new church is formed by people from the parent congregation itself.

---

times it is more feasible to be specific and ask those who live in a certain area to form the nucleus. My friend Kent Tucker started Grace Church, Aurora, Colorado, in that manner. He was invited by South Presbyterian Church of Denver to form a nucleus for a new church, so he began by plotting the residences of church members on a wall map of the Denver area. When he did, he was impressed at the unusually thick concentration of pins in the suburb of Aurora. This helped him decide both whom to recruit for the nucleus and where to locate the church.

Kent Tucker's nucleus was 60 in size. This is somewhat larger than the average of 43 that showed up in a recent *Leadership* journal survey.[1] It is considerably smaller, however, than some nuclei that have been sent out by Paul

Yonggi Cho, pastor of the Yoido Full Gospel Church of Seoul, Korea. In a pastors letter, Cho says: "I have sent three of my associate ministers to other areas to start their own churches. Yet these faithful ministers were not sent out empty-handed. We gave each of them a starting congregation of 5,000 members plus the necessary funds to have a successful ministry in their area."[2] I once asked Cho how much money he gave them, and he said between $1.5 and $4 million (U.S.) each. He told me that his brother, Cho Young Mook, was one who received $4 million in 1984 and that his church was approaching 100,000 members in 1989. Nine other churches are running between 10,000 and 30,000 members each. I mention this in passing because I think that Cho has set some world records for hiving off.

In some cases the nucleus can be formed around a special interest group that has previously existed in the parent church. A common example these days is a group that prefers a contemporary worship style while the parent church's philosophy of ministry is more traditional. If God so leads, such a group can become the church planting nucleus and start a new church that can likely reach out and win individuals in the community whom the traditional church was not previously reaching.

2. Colonization. Colonization is a more radical form of hiving off. In colonization the new church is planted in a different geographical area, meaning that the nucleus members will make a move and find new homes, new jobs, and new schools in the target community. I saw this happen right here in Pasadena, California, when back in 1984 four couples left the Covenant Life Church home base for apostolic church planter Larry Tomczak in Gaithersburg, Maryland, and moved to Pasadena to plant the Abundant Life Community Church. My friend Che Ahn came as senior pastor, and they have grown to almost 500.

Colonization and Commitment

The colonization method of church planting presupposes such a high level of Christian commitment to the Great Commission that some are surprised it functions at all. Many existing churches would no more expect their church members to do this than they would expect to receive $4 million from Paul Yonggi Cho. But it does happen, and its frequency has been increasing throughout the decade of the 1980s, particularly among baby boomers.

James Feeney of Abbott Loop Christian Center in Anchorage, Alaska, has written a book on this, *Church Planting by the Team Method*. Abbott Loop began colonizing in 1967, and by 1987 they had planted 40 existing churches (plus 15 that did not survive). Those churches in turn had planted 17 others. In 1987, 10 of the original 40 churches were surveyed. The 137 people who originally moved out to colonize those 10 churches had grown to 2,068.[3] The last time I was in touch with Jim Feeney he was preparing a team of 15 adults to move with him from Anchorage to Medford, Oregon, where they would be joined by four couples from a church he had previously planted near New York City.

Most of the colonizing churches of which I am aware are charismatic. However the most aggressive of them all may be the noncharismatic Boston Church of Christ pioneered by Kip McKean. I am aware that some of the methods used by the Boston Church of Christ to promote commitment and discipleship have come under criticism, but their track record for planting new churches clearly deserves mention. In the first eight years (1982-1990) through the colonization method they planted new churches or restructured old ones in such places as Chicago, London, New York, Cairo, Toronto, Johannesburg, Paris, Stockholm, Bombay, Kingston, San Francisco, Atlanta, Mexico

City, Buenos Aires, Hong Kong, Los Angeles, Manila and Tokyo. Many of these churches have in turn planted other churches, totaling 70 churches related to the Boston church. Their cumulative Sunday attendance is over 30,000—not including the 4,500 in Boston.

3. Adoption. Church adoption, like human adoption, means that someone else gives birth but the child becomes part of your family. I first heard of this some years ago at Melodyland Christian Center in Anaheim, California. It seems that some believers from St. Louis had visited the services in Melodyland and they liked what they saw so much that they felt St. Louis needed a similar ministry. So on their own initiative they pioneered a work in St. Louis using the Melodyland philosophy of ministry. Word got back to Melodyland, they established contact with the young church, and offered to help them in every way. A family-type relationship was subsequently formed, and Melodyland functioned as a parent church.

Grace Community Church of Panorama City, California, at one point decided to do their extension ministry through adoption. Pastor John MacArthur recruited seminary students and brought them on his staff as interns. By the time they had graduated they had fully absorbed the Grace Community Church philosophy of Bible ministry. As the pulpits of independent Bible churches in California and other states became vacant, the interns would candidate. When they received a call, the church was then adopted into Grace Community's informal family of churches. Through adoption several of these churches have now been revitalized. I previously mentioned that it was easier to have babies than to raise the dead, but, through adoption, John MacArthur and his interns have been used to raise several churches from the dead.

4. *Accidental parenthood.* Now that birth control is widespread, the timing of many births is planned by the parents. Even so, accidents still happen, and some new babies were not carefully planned. I speak from experience, because of the three girls born to my wife, Doris, and me, only one was planned. But the upshot is that we love them all just the same.

So far the methods of church planting that I have described are all planned. But accidents do happen in churches as well, and sometimes the nucleus for a new church will break off from the parent church for reasons better described as carnal than as spiritual. Donald McGavran and George Hunter say, "Sometimes over a theological shootout, personality conflict, leadership struggle, or disagreement on priorities, a congregation will split. One faction will pull out, start another congregation, and both congregations will prosper more than the one former church did."[4]

What can we say to this phenomenon? I'm sure that God does not approve of church splits or the causes of them listed by McGavran and Hunter. Nor would I want to go on record as advocating church splitting as a church planting methodology. It is much better to pray and plan and minister in harmony. Nevertheless, when the dust settles, I have to believe that God loves both of the resulting churches and accepts them as part of the bride of Christ. Just as God can be glorified through the healing of a man born blind, He can be glorified through the offspring of accidental church parenthood.

The Parent and the Child
5. *The satellite model.* The four church planting methods I have described so far: hiving off, colonization, adoption, and accidental parenthood, all result in the new

church gaining autonomy from the parent church. The satellite model is different in that by design the new congregations are only semiautonomous. They continue to have an organic relationship with the parent church. Sometimes they are called annexes or branch churches. In most cases the senior pastor of the mother or central church functions as the senior pastor of each of the satellites.

Worldwide the satellite model is having a very powerful impact for the spread of the gospel. John Vaughan reports his extensive research on the subject in his book *The Large Church*. He says, "Large churches with satellite groups combine the best of two growth strategies....Although many of these churches are committed to building a large central church, most are just as committed to penetrating and reaching the city through the use of small groups coordinated fully, in most instances, by the parent congregation."[5]

The second largest church in the world, the Jotabeche Methodist Pentecostal Church of Santiago, Chile, has grown through planting satellites. The central sanctuary, where Pastor Javier Vasquez preaches on Sunday nights, holds only 16,000 and by itself is grossly inadequate for the 350,000 or so members. But throughout the city of Santiago over 40 satellites with their own church buildings and congregations numbering up to several thousands are in full swing. While each one enjoys a certain autonomy, they nevertheless consider themselves part of the Jotabeche Church and under the pastoral leadership of Javier Vasquez.

Satellite churches are flourishing in Chile and Brazil and Nigeria and the Philippines, but several are also becoming prominent in the United States. Perhaps the national leader is Pastor Lee Roberson of the Highland Park Baptist Church in Chattanooga, Tennessee. A recent report I received stated that the weekly attendance of that church was 9,000:

4,000 in the mother church and 5,000 in 60 satellites called "chapels."

My friend Randy Pope pioneered a Presbyterian Church of America in Atlanta, which he called Perimeter Church, named after the freeway encircling Atlanta. The church bulletin says, "Perimeter Church is one church with many congregations. All of Perimeter's congregations come together four times a year for very special worship services called *Combined Celebrations*." Randy Pope cares for the Metro Congregation and the satellites are called East Congregation, Intown Congregation and Northwest Congregation.

I like to call these kinds of satellites "scattered satellites" because they are located off the campus of the parent church. It is possible also to have "gathered satellites" in which the semiautonomous satellite congregations actually meet on the same grounds as the parent congregation. Although there are exceptions, most of the gathered satellites turn out to be congregations of different cultural groupings, and they could better be described in the next category of multicongregational churches.

6. *Multicongregational churches.* By definition, multicongregational churches minister to several different ethnic groups. If properly managed, they are very effective in urban areas where many different minority groups live in geographical proximity to each other. Some multicongregational churches simply share facilities with ethnic congregations that maintain their own autonomy, while others go so far as to share the entire church administration equitably.

The best example I have found of the latter is Temple Baptist Church of Los Angeles, pioneered by my friend Jim Conklin. Let me hasten to say that not every pastor is equipped to handle a multicongregational church. It requires one who has a special ability for cross-cultural ministry, which I call the missionary gift. Jim Conklin has the gift. He is a veteran missionary to Thailand and has earned the Doctor of Missiology degree from Fuller Seminary. He knows both theory and practice.

For years before retiring in 1988, Jim Conklin was the senior pastor of an English-language congregation and

The biblical prototype of a catalytic church planter was the apostle Paul. When Paul went to a new place he did what was necessary to get a church started but he didn't usually stay there very long.

coordinating pastor over a Hispanic congregation, a Filipino congregation and a Burmese congregation. The ethnic pastors of those congregations are members of the staff. A church coordinating council has representatives from each of the congregations. Each congregation contributes to the church a share of operational costs according to their weekly usage of so many square feet of the church buildings, eliminating any possible accusation of paternalism. Each Sunday each congregation holds services in its own language, but once a quarter they all worship together in "The Sounds of Heaven." Temple Church projects planting other ethnic congregations and bringing them into fellowship with the others.

7. *The multiple campus model.* At the beginning of this chapter I affirmed that all 12 of these methods work.

This is true of the multiple campus model, but not as true as the other 11. The concept here is that one local congregation, led by the same staff, with one membership roll and one budget owns and occupies two or more church properties, holding weekly worship services at more than one.

In one sense it could be argued that buying or building another church location for the same church is not church planting at all. On the other hand, multiple campuses have at times begun as the same church but ended up as separate churches. For several years, for example, Scott Memorial Church of San Diego, California, met on three locations: San Diego, El Cajon, and North San Diego. The preaching staff would rotate so that no one would know ahead of time which pastor would preach at which location. And the church grew first under the leadership of Tim La Haye and then under David Jeremiah. Eventually, however, it was deemed wiser to have three churches.

The jury is still out as to whether the multiple campus model is a desirable long range plan for a church. Two of the nation's largest churches are currently using it. Pastors Paul Walker of Mt. Paran Church of God in Atlanta and Jack Hayford of The Church On The Way in Van Nuys, California, are preaching in two locations on Sunday mornings and reporting excellent results. As I learn of more successful models, I may be able to recommend it more enthusiastically.

SODALITY MODELS

If the focus of the modality model is the local church, the focus of the sodality model is outside of the local church in a separate agency. At this point I am restricting my use of sodality to either a denominational agency or a parachurch organization. I listed seven methods under modality models, and here I will list the other five.

8. *The mission team.* A very common way of planting new churches is for a church planting agency to recruit, finance, and sponsor a team of workers to plant a new church.

In the first chapter I mentioned the PRAXIS program of the Southern Baptist Home Mission Board in which they recruit seminary students for a 10-week church planting field seminar. Southern Baptists have also had success in recruiting church planting teams of college students for the Summer vacations.

In their excellent book, *Creating Communities of the Kingdom,* David Shenk and Ervin Stutzman go so far as to argue that "a team is essential for church planting."[6] They point out that the team in one sense is already a church, that the members are diverse enough to contribute complimentary gifts, and that a special chemistry called *synergy* occurs, which dramatically increases the efficiency of each individual on the team.

9. *The catalytic church planter.* God gifts and calls some very special people as catalytic church planters. Their ministry is to go into a new area, develop a nucleus for a new church, and then move on and do it again. The biblical prototype of a catalytic church planter was the apostle Paul, who said, "According to the grace of God which was given to me, as a wise master builder I have laid the foundation, and another builds on it. But let each one take heed how he builds on it" (1 Cor. 3:10, *NKJV*). When Paul went to a new place he did what was necessary to get a church started but he didn't usually stay there very long.

Catalytic church planters are invaluable, especially when working with a denominational church planting agency. One of the most effective catalytic church planters I have met is Harold Cameron, a Southern Baptist who spent many years working with the Illinois State Baptist Association. He is now retired, but during his ministry he started or personally supervised the planting of over 500 new churches. It would usually take him about eight weeks to organize the nucleus to the point where they were ready to call their first pastor.

I once asked Harold how he did it. "Oh," he said, "I do it through the telephone. I go to a phone booth with three rolls of dimes and if I don't have a nucleus by the time my money runs out, I consider it a resistant area and move on elsewhere!" He, of course, had his tongue in his cheek as he told me that, but the general principle holds. He saw his role as getting in and getting out as quickly as possible. As I will mention again later, one of the common mistakes in church planting is to spend an excessive amount of time in building the nucleus.

Not that it can or should always be done in eight weeks. For many a four to six month period is more realistic. One friend, Bill Putman, who spent years as a catalytic church planter with the Churches of Christ, planned on a year and a half to develop a strong nucleus before he and his family would move on to do it again.

Founders, Tentmakers, and Other Planters

10. *The founding pastor.* The founding pastor is sent out by the agency not only to build the nucleus but to pastor the new church for an indefinite period of time. This is perhaps the most commonly used sodality model for starting churches.

Sometimes the founding pastor will sense a lifetime call to the new church. I first became aware of this years ago when my friend Robert Schuller told me that when he came to California in 1955 to plant what is now the Crystal Cathedral, he knew then that God had given him his lifetime ministry. Likewise Schuller's neighbor, Rick Warren. As Rick was finishing his work in Southwestern Baptist Theological Seminary, he prayed, "I'll go anywhere you send me, Lord, but please allow me to spend my whole life wherever that may be." I have since heard him say in public that although he is not yet 40, Saddleback Valley Community Church is his last parish.

Some founding pastors also regard themselves as "lead pastors." The plan is that they will start the church and pastor it at least for a time. Certain lead pastors feel that their principal gift is evangelism, and that in the early years of a new church their ministry can be quite effective. But as the church matures it will need a leader with gifts of pastoring rather than evangelism, so a change is in order. Others may have pastoral gifts, but they frankly recognize that God has equipped them to pastor a small church. If it becomes apparent that the growth potential is there for the church to become a large church, they will voluntarily step aside for another pastor better equipped for large church ministry.

Frequently the founding pastor is bivocational or a tentmaker. This is one of the major ways of cutting the costs of new church development, and I highly recommend it. Most growing denominations make good use of bivocational workers. Southern Baptists, for example, have 10,000 bivocational pastors in the United States. They nurture these workers by giving them special recognition, providing them services they need, and training them in tracks that bypass the traditional seminary system. A full 50 percent of Southern Baptist pastors are not college graduates. This is a key reason why the Southern Baptist Convention is the largest Protestant denomination in the nation.[7]

Keep in mind that bivocational pastors can see their status as either permanent or temporary. The majority of the

Southern Baptist bivocational pastors regard themselves as permanent pastors of small, frequently rural, churches. On the other hand, the majority of founding pastors see their bivocational status as only temporary until the new church has a sufficient budget to cover their salary. Most plan to quit their secular job and give full time to the church as soon as they possibly can.

11. The independent church planter. Independent church planters go out on their own to start new churches. They do not serve either a denominational or a parachurch agency. In the strict use of the term, this is not a sodality model except for the fact that these independent church planters constitute themselves as a sort of sodality. Many independent church planters have done well in recent years, but their procedures do not differ enough from others of the 12 methods to merit more than a mention at this point.

12. The apostolic church planter. In recent years a new and very effective model for planting new churches has been developing chiefly within the independent charismatic movement. Many charismatics believe that all the New Testament spiritual gifts, including the gift of apostle, are operative today. Those who are recognized as apostles function with much the same spiritual authority as did the apostle Paul. Sometimes they are called apostles and sometimes other titles are used, but their role is the same.

Many apostles have been founding pastors of new churches themselves; they work in team ministry, and they use their local church as a base for church planting operations. When the local church is the base, this model combines both modality and sodality characteristics. Usually the church planters emerge from the congregation itself. The apostle confirms their call to full-time ministry, trains them, ordains them, and sends them out to plant a church. The new church is typically not a satellite, but an autonomous church. It has its own legal standing and owns its own property. However, the pastor and the church remain under the ultimate authority of the apostle. The apostle's authority, therefore, is not a legal authority but a spiritual authority. Only the Holy Spirit produces and sustains the relationship. As the number of churches under one apostle increases they relate to each other much as they would in a denomination. They typically reject the idea of denominationalism, however, because bureaucratic denominations are seen as legal (not spiritual) organizations. Terms such as "apostolic network" or "fellowship" or "movement" are preferred to "denomination" although their sociological function is similar.

There is some overlap between the apostolic church planter model and the colonization model described above. Four of the leaders of these new apostolic networks, Larry Tomczak of People of Destiny International, Dick Benjamin of Abbott Loop Christian Center, Terry Edwards of Harvest Field World Missions, and Jim Durkin of Gospel Outreach have collaborated in an excellent introduction to this methodology, *The Church Planter's Handbook*. They are all advocating colonization as the preferred method. Larry Tomczak's chapter "Relationship with the Sending Church" is a good place to start for those who wish to understand the biblical basis of this particular philosophy of ministry. He shows "how various churches and leaders can be related relationally and organically, not necessarily legally and organizationally."[8]

The church planting method you choose will depend on your gifts, sense of God's leading and relationships with a local church or parachurch agency. Whichever one of these approaches you take, the planning stage continues as you determine what kind of church you are planting—its target audience, location and size.

NOTES
1. Dean Merrill, "Mothering a New Church," *Leadership* (Winter, 1985), p. 100.
2. Paul Yonggi Cho, December 1983 Pastors Letter, p. 1.
3. James H. Feeney, *Church Planting by the Team Method* (Anchorage, AK: Abbott Loop Christian Center, 1988), p. 43.
4. Donald A. McGavran and George Hunter III, *Church Growth Strategies that Work* (Nashville, TN: Abingdon Press, 1980), p. 115.
5. John N. Vaughan, *The Large Church* (Grand Rapids, MI: Baker Book House, 1985), p. 23.
6. David W. Shenk and Ervin R. Stutzman, *Creating Communities of the Kingdom: New Testament Models of Church Planting* (Scottdale, PA: Herald Press, 1988), p. 44.
7. For more information on bivocational pastors in the Southern Baptist Convention see Luther M. Dorr, *The Bivocational Pastor* (Nashville, TN: Broadman Press, 1988).
8. Dick Benjamin, Jim Durkin, Terry Edwards, and Larry Tomczak, *The Church Planter's Handbook* (South Lake Tahoe, CA: Christian Equippers Int., 1988), p. 105.

5

THE LOCATION: A CRUCIAL DECISION

Nothing will be more influential on the success or failure of your church planting project than proper site selection. It is well worth whatever time, energy and money it takes to develop a sound feasibility study. A good location will cover a multitude of blunders. A poor location will accentuate them. Jack Redford, who for years headed up the national church planting efforts for Southern Baptists, feels so strongly about this that he says, "Failure to obtain full and complete facts on a neighborhood or community prior to launching a new congregation may be just like signing the death warrant long before the new work has been started."[1]

YOUR FIRST DECISION

Where will the new church be planted? Your first decision in response to this question concerns your starting point. In planning for new church development either of two starting points is legitimate:

1. *You start with the geographical location.* Say, for example, you feel that God has called you to plant a church in south Dallas or Pumphandle, Nebraska. Your first step, then, must be to go to the area and do a feasibility study in order to find out your options for target audiences.

2. *You start with the target audience.* Say, for example, that God has called you to plant a church for coal miners or for Filipinos or for yuppies. Your first step in this case is to find out where the target audience is located and what your options are for geographical areas.

The Cross-Cultural Issue

Part and parcel to this process is the decision as to whether you feel God is calling you to monocultural ministry or cross-cultural ministry. Particularly since the 1960s Christian idealism has often clouded common sense in making this choice. The Christian community, rightly so, has been developing a growing compassion for the poor, the oppressed, the minorities, the homeless, and the handicapped. God loves these people and desires that churches be planted among them. But He obviously does not call everyone to do it. If you have compassion on people in a different socio-cultural group from your own, be sure that your decision to plant a church among them comes from God and not from your human emotions.

I do not want to be misunderstood. I believe in and practice cross-cultural ministry. For 16 years I lived in Bolivia as a cross-cultural missionary and for almost another 20 years I have taught on a missiological faculty where our stock in trade is training for cross-cultural ministries. But I also realize that God has not made everyone else like He made me. I believe I have a special spiritual gift for this ministry called the missionary gift, which I have explained in detail in my book *Your Spiritual Gifts Can Help Your Church Grow*.[2] But my studies suggest that God has given this gift to something like 1 percent of the Body of Christ.

The pure and simple fact is that most pastors are monocultural. They have been called and equipped by God to minister primarily to those of their own people group. Most Korean pastors minister best to Koreans. Most Russian pastors minister best to Russians. Most American black pastors

---

The overwhelming odds are that God will call you and equip you to plant a church among people who are pretty much like yourself.

---

minister best to American blacks. Most Mexican pastors minister best to Mexicans. Most yuppie pastors minister best to yuppies.

What does this mean? If God calls you to plant a new church He may give you a missionary gift, and He may call you to plant a church in a different people group as He did me. But the overwhelming odds are that He will call you and equip you to plant a church among people who are pretty much like yourself.

Cross-cultural church planting is such a specialized field, and there is so little interest in it across the board, that I am not going to deal with it in any detail in this book. This does not mean it is unimportant. Certainly with the rapidly increasing multiethnic composition of our American society, cross-cultural church planting is of utmost importance. I have expressed my own strong feelings on the matter in my essay "Evangelizing the Real America."[3] For those who are interested in more information, the books I most recommend are David Hesselgrave's *Planting Churches Cross-Culturally*,[4] Jerry Appleby's *Missions Have Come Home to America*,[5] and Charles Brock's *The Principles and Practice of Indigenous Church Planting.*[6]

Geography and Culture

Most church planters select their target audience first and then search out a geographical location appropriate for reaching them. If this is your choice, keep in mind that sometimes geography and culture coincide and sometimes they do not.

One of the best examples of culture and geography coinciding would be an Indian reservation. Navajos are found in abundance on the Navajo Reservation, but very few are found across an invisible line in the Hopi Reservation, or in Marietta, Georgia. Likewise there are some urban areas that have a higher than average concentration of certain people groups. In the Los Angeles area, for example, I know I will find many Samoans in Compton, Chinese in Monterey Park, Koreans in Koreatown, and yuppies in Mission Viejo.

In most American urban areas, however, geography and culture do not coincide. Webs of human relationships often supersede geographical boundaries. Social networks play a powerful role in human behavior. Why is it that so many Americans drive past a half dozen churches before they get to the church they attend? Why don't Christian people attend the church closest to home? The major factor, although it is not the only one, is that they will travel almost any distance so long as they find at their destination people from their own social network. Social ties are more important to them than geographical locations.

This is why the parish system where the ministry area of a local church is limited to prescribed geographical boundaries may have been useful centuries ago in relatively stable homogenous societies, but is dysfunctional in today's mobile urban mosaic.

All this means that when you select a site for the new church, locate it in a place where the members of the social networks of your target audience or audiences can most easily get together.

DEMOGRAPHICS

The indispensable foundation for intelligent selection of the site for the new church is demographics. Fortunately our high-tech age has made sophisticated demographic information readily accessible to church planters who are anything but specialists in the population sciences.

Before looking at the sources of demographic data, it will be well to understand why we need to do a demographic study as part of our church planting process. There are three main reasons for doing it:

1. *Identifying target audiences.* Demographics will help you know who lives where and how many there are. Discovering who lives in a given area is extremely helpful for planning ministry. In any geographical territory will be found different people groups, homogeneous units, "ethclasses," life-style groups, social networks or whatever term one wishes to use to describe the target audience.

2. *Determining receptivity.* Skillful use of demographic information can help you estimate beforehand the degree of receptivity the members of the target audience will have to your methods of sharing the gospel. Mobility data are very

helpful because people just moving in are ordinarily more receptive than those who have lived there a long time. Also through demographics you can discover some of the people's felt needs, particularly those that through your ministry you can help meet. If you help meet people's needs, they frequently become very receptive to your message.

3. *Building confidence.* A good feasibility study with up-to-date demographics builds confidence on three sides. For one thing it impresses those who are sponsoring you for

---

When you select a site for the new church, locate it in a place where the members of the social networks of your target audience or audiences can most easily get together.

---

the church planting activity. For another it impresses those who are considering becoming members of the nucleus or the new church. They are enthusiastic about following a leader who has the expertise to know their community that well. And last but not least it will build your own self-confidence. You will feel that you have a handle on the harvest and your decision making will be ever so much easier.

I said that good demographics are indispensable. But I will be the first to admit that there are exceptions to the rule. I recall that in the late '70s my church, Lake Avenue Congregational Church of Pasadena, California, decided to plant a new church called Sunrise Community Church. They hired John Wimber, then of the Charles E. Fuller Institute of Evangelism and Church Growth to do a feasibility study. The cost of getting that demographic information together (it was more expensive than it is now) was around $6,000.

While this was going on, my wife, Doris, and I were at a dinner party with Jack Hayford of Church On The Way and his wife, Anna. Over dinner I told him that we were planting a new church.

"Oh," he said, "that's interesting. We're planting a new church also. Ours will be in Valencia."

It occurred to me to ask him how it was he chose Valencia as the site for the new church.

He replied, "It was quite simple. I was driving through the area one day, simply on call, when suddenly I felt a deep passion for the people living there. It was profoundly moving, and with it the Holy Spirit clearly spoke to me: 'Plant a church in Valencia.'"

I laughed out loud and said, "Jack, not only is it more fun to be a Pentecostal than a Congregationalist, it's also a lot cheaper!"

If the Holy Spirit speaks to you directly about where He wants the church, do it His way. If not, what I have said still holds: good demographics are indispensable.

WHERE IS THE INFORMATION?

I am going to list 12 sources of demographic information. Number 12 is by far the best, but I would not advise you to skip the first 11. Your knowledge of your target community and its people will increase in direct proportion to the time and energy you expend in going to these sources. By visiting offices and talking to people you are able to get in touch with attitudes and feelings that no computerized report could duplicate. Many jewels of insight are collected through casual conversations rather than through formal studies.

Digging out demographics is like mining gold. Prospectors find a likely place and dig a tunnel. If they find a vein of gold, wonderful, but more often than not they don't. So they dig another tunnel and another until they do find it. Depending on the time and place, some of these sources will give you very little useful information. If so, go on to the next. Eventually you will strike gold and get the demographic information you need. Persistence will pay.

1. *U.S. census data.* Our government takes a thorough population census every 10 years in the year ending with zero. The closer you are to the year when the last census data was published, the more valuable it is. This mass of information is available to all U.S. citizens. You can get it for a state, a county, a standard metropolitan statistical area, a census tract, a block group or an individual block. Each region has a government-designated agency that handles and distributes this material, and you will need to ask around to discover which agency distributes yours. You can get computer printouts or even floppy disks to use on your own personal computer.

Keep in mind that census data is both raw and digested. The floppy disks, for example, contain raw data, and I have met very few church planters who have the ability to handle raw census data. Ask your census agency for any digested data they might have prepared: maps, graphs, charts, summary reports and the like. These will be much more useful to you.

2. *City or county planning commissions.* Most larger cities and their respective counties have planning commissions. Some of these are rather informal and uninformed groups of citizens, but others have developed sophisticated offices and staffs. In order to do their long range planning, these commissions need to use digested census data along with other information. You will come up dry in some cases, but you may well strike gold here. I know of county planning offices where the pertinent demographic information has been carefully classified, refined, displayed with excellent graphic skill and published at reasonable prices for the general public. Many church planters can find the bulk of what they need for their feasibility study right here.

My friend Pastor Clay Perkins of Piedmont Christian Church in Greensboro, North Carolina went to his city planning office to see what they might have. He found to his delight that the city planner was a committed Christian. Not only did the city planner, Art Davis, give Perkins the information he needed, but he volunteered to do a series of three seminars for all the interested pastors in the city.

3. School boards. In order to qualify for government educational grants, many school boards need to keep up-to-date demographic files on their districts. Since they are public agencies, they technically should share their information with church planters or anyone else who can use it. Much of what you get from a school board, however, may depend on the individual or individuals you deal with. Some consider themselves harassed and will not be very helpful. Others, however, will provide you with excellent material for your feasibility study.

4. Public utilities. Local electric companies, gas companies, water companies and telephone companies depend on knowing population trends in the area for planning future business. In many cases these businesses are private, so obtaining access to their planning data may depend heavily on personal contacts.

5. Local universities. If you have a university in your city or your area, a visit to their sociology department could pay rich dividends. It may be that they have a recent masters thesis or similar document on the demographics of your area. If they cannot help you directly, they frequently can give you leads that otherwise you might not have been aware of.

Banks, Radio Stations and More

6. *Lending institutions.* Banks, savings and loans and finance companies frequently keep their planning information close to their chest. However, it is well to be aware of this possibility and move in to any opening that the Lord may provide you there.

7. *Chambers of commerce.* Some may wonder why I did not put the chamber of commerce first on the list. It is because the quality of demographic information found there is so spotty. Some chambers of commerce are more like municipal advertising agencies, but others provide serious planning information for those in the area or those who wish to move into the area. Don't fail to try your chamber of commerce.

8. *Radio stations.* In order to sell advertising, radio stations gather demographic information for their listening area. Up until recently the federal government required the stations to provide this material upon request. This has since been changed, but many will do it just to maintain good public relations.

9. *Public libraries.* You may find it a tedious process to try to dig pertinent demographic information out of your local public library. On the other hand, this may be your most fruitful source. If you are fortunate to find a skilled research librarian who is somewhat bored and looking for an exciting research challenge, you may have someone who will practically do your feasibility study for you. A well-placed box of candy may turn out to be an excellent investment.

10. *Real estate firms.* Real estate firms, especially the larger ones, have access to extensive demographic data. Since you are planting a church and presumably will eventually be looking for land in the area, consider becoming a client of a real estate agent while you are still in your planning phase. Explain carefully that you may not need the property for some time, but assure the agent that you will use them whenever the time does come. If you can form a good relationship, it will open the door to whatever information they have.

11. *Newspapers.* Particularly in metropolitan areas, reading the daily newspaper will give you valuable information. This is a long-term process, but it will usually pay off. Through the years I have found extremely useful information in the *Los Angeles Times* that I have shared with many church planters.

12. *Commercial geodemographics.* I have saved commercial geodemographics for last, and am dealing with it in a category apart from the other 11 sources of demographic information. Even five years ago, few could have dreamed of the sophisticated demographic information that our high-tech information age would make available to church planters.

Geodemographics is a science developed particularly for marketing. Church planting is obviously a form of marketing, even though some church leaders still emotionally deny that marketing has any place at all in the kingdom of God. I see marketing as neutral as, for example, video cameras or cellular telephones or airplanes or word processors. They are tools available to contemporary society that can be used for the glory of God or otherwise, depending on who is using them.

Our national geodemographic industry is coordinated through a large computer complex in Ithaca, New York.

Using U.S. census data as a foundation, information is constantly updated through multiple sources of ongoing population studies so that its current accuracy is excellent now and getting better all the time. Several companies draw from that data and package it in forms that make it useful to clients whose success or failure in their endeavor depends significantly on having access to pertinent population facts.

Church Information and Development Services

While many secular companies can provide valuable information for church planters, the data provided is in relatively undigested formats. It is particularly useful for industrial marketing managers who are specially trained to use and apply it. The average church planter or pastor does not have this expertise, so more help is needed. Fortunately a company has been formed to take the commercial geodemographic data and package it specifically for church leaders. It is called Church Information and Development Services (CIDS) of 3001 Redhill Avenue, Suite 2-220, Costa Mesa, CA 92626-9664 (800-442-6277). The president, Michael B. Regele (pronounced "Regal") fully understands pastors' needs since he is a Fuller Seminary graduate, a Presbyterian minister, and a skilled church consultant.

You can request your demographic data from CIDS by providing them the intersection of any two streets in the U.S.A. and the radius or radii around that intersection that you consider your ministry area. In a short turn-around time and for a reasonable price (well within the budget of most church planters) they will send you their "Ministry Area Profile," which will include a Pop-Facts report, a Demographic Trends summary, a Vision Area Profile and one or more color-plotted maps of the ministry area. You can order maps to highlight valuable information such as projected 5-year population growth in different sections of your area, household income, median age, black population, Hispanic population or baby boomer population.

One of the most valuable maps will show you where primary vision segments live. The Vision Area Profile above is based on a scientific market segment analysis that has classified the U.S. population into 50 life-style groups. Each one has a descriptive name and a concise summary of this target audience's characteristics. Some of the market segments are called White Picket Fence, Hard Years, Metro Ethnic Mix, Living Off the Land, Good Family Life, Sunset Years, Successful Singles and Establishing Roots.

I cannot recommend too highly using the CIDS Vision Area Profile in your planning phase. To put it simply, no church in America can minister effectively to all 50 life-style groups. The idealism of many young church planters causes them to dream of reaching, if not all 50 groups, at least a large proportion of them. This is a sure recipe for frustration. The fact of the matter is that most churches whether rural, urban or suburban will find that God has equipped them to reach effectively one or two or three or possibly a couple more of these groups. The larger the church, the broader the spectrum it can serve, but even superchurches find their market ranges of ministry limited. The value of the Vision Area Profile is to help you seek the mind of the Lord as to which ones of the 50 life-style segments He has called you and equipped you to serve. If you do this and do it well, your chances of receiving God's blessing for a healthy, thriving church are enormously increased.

CIDS services for churches are expanding rapidly. Ask them about their New Church Development Site Study. This package includes comprehensive demographic reports, up to 20 color plotted maps and an analysis report. Additional options include on-site review of the area, interviews with community leaders and church officials and consultation with the client.

What to Ask For

Let me say once again that while you may find a relatively small amount of money invested in geodemographic services paying you large dividends, don't allow it to become a shortcut. You will do well to track down as many of the other 11 sources of demographic data as you possibly can.

When you walk into a given office, it is best to know ahead of time what to ask for. Sometimes a helpful person in the office will volunteer information. Frequently, however, overworked employees will give you what you ask for and nothing else. Here is a list of five kinds of information that will be very helpful to you:

1. *The socio-cultural composition of the area and the locations and sizes of the different socio-cultural groups.* While not all will be able to provide this, most will understand what you are asking for.

2. *Population growth projections for the area in general and for specific census tracts within the area.* It is true that CIDS will provide this, but by asking the questions you may receive valuable local information that has not as yet reached the CIDS computers.

3. *Internal migration patterns.* Find out where people are moving out and where they are moving in. If you are targeting an urban area you will particularly want to know which are the ethnically changing communities and what is going on there.

4. *Traffic patterns.* Studies are constantly being made about how many vehicles travel on which streets or roads in an area. If you can locate these, you can get a good indication of where your church might best be located.

Remember, people's Sunday driving patterns follow their weekday patterns.

5. *Land use projections.* Particularly in growing sections of the country certain urban reserve areas have been designated for development two years or five years or more from now. While you may not see many people moving in today, tomorrow there may be massive residential development. Certain individuals know this quite well ahead of time, and it will help you to know it also.

Religious Data

Unfortunately for American church planters, the U.S. Census Bureau refuses to ask religious questions. Data on religious affiliation are much less accessible than population characteristics in general.

The most recommendable source for this information is the Yellow Pages. Not all of the churches in the area are listed in the Yellow Pages, but most of them will be. Councils of churches and chambers of commerce at times have church listings, but in most cases they will be much less complete than the Yellow Pages. This will give you a fix on the number of churches in the area and their approximate location, which is one of the first things you will want to know.

You will also want to know who and how many people go to these churches, which will then allow you to calculate the approximate number of unchurched in your target area. The best way I know of obtaining this information is by using the telephone. I suggest that you, or people you can get to help you, call as many churches as possible and talk to whoever answers the phone. Here are the questions to ask. Keep them simple and uncomplicated:

1. What is your approximate membership? Or if the church is one that does not count members as such: More or less how many adults would you say consider your church as their primary source of spiritual ministry?

2. What is your approximate Sunday morning worship attendance currently running?

3. What is your sanctuary's approximate seating capacity?

   Following this, try to get some information that will give you an idea of growth rates:

4. If you have _____ members now, would you say that you had more or less five years ago? Could you guess how many?

5. If you have _____ in attendance now, would you say that you had more or less five years ago? Could you guess how many?

   Since the names of the churches you find in the Yellow Pages do not always tell you what denomination it belongs to, ask:

6. Is your church a part of a denomination? Which one?

   People will frequently fudge on this final question, but try to get information on the ethnic makeup of the church:

7. What are the principal ethnic groups your church serves? Could you guess the relative proportion of each?

In order to calculate the unchurched in your area you will admittedly have to use a measure of approximations, guesswork and extrapolations. Your telephone survey will give you a good basis on which to do this. The ten-year *Churches and Church Membership in the United States 1980*[7] published by a consortium of church groups will give you their best estimate of the number of unchurched in your county. Do not expect pinpoint accuracy, but for most counties it is a good ballpark figure to work with.

CHOOSING THE REAL ESTATE

Eventually (but not too soon, as I will explain later), you will have to choose a piece of real estate for your new church. There are many imponderables in doing this. Subjective judgments play a strong role. Availability is frequently a restricting factor. Cost is a major consideration. Zoning regulations make some otherwise desirable locations less desirable. There are many variables that change from case to case.

There are, however, three considerations that should be given high priority in all cases:

1. *Visibility.* If at all possible, be sure that unchurched people, the more the better, can see your church. People in the community should be able to recognize and identify your church building. Is it worth paying extra for visibility? Here is what Methodist church planting expert Ezra Earl Jones says: "While many churches seek to save money by locating a half block or more off a main street where property values are lower, the visibility that is lost costs more

than the savings on land."[8] Even 100 feet one way or another can make a big difference. This is where your traffic pattern information should be used.

2. *Accessibility.* In most cases good visibility will provide good accessibility, but not always. Be sure people can get to your church easily. Some churches with good visibility from a freeway or an interstate are so difficult to find through surface streets that the accessibility nullifies the visibility. Robert Schuller says, "It is obvious that the best product cannot be sold and will not be bought if people can't get their hands on it!"[9]

3. *Size.* Many church planters make the mistake of looking for a property adequate for the church as it is now rather than large enough for what God wants the church to be. Growth has all too often been stifled by shortsightedness at this point. The rule of thumb is to look for three-fourths to one acre per 100 adults who will be part of your church of the future. This means that for a church of 300 adults you will want 2 to 3 acres; for 800, 5 to 8 acres; and for 2,400, 16 to 24 acres.

Some of the variables for this decision include the driving habits of your people (how many per car?), availability of off-campus parking, number of services possible, and city codes for landscaping. Pray that God will give you a special measure of faith and vision as you decide on the size of your property.

As you reach the end of your feasibility study, you should have the answers to a number of basic questions about your new church: What kind of people will make up this church? Where are they? How will you reach out to them? You may even have your eye on a piece of land at this stage. The important thing is that you have enough information to move ahead with confidence: it's time to begin the actual work of planting a church.

NOTES
1. Jack Redford, *Planting New Churches* (Nashville, TN: Broadman Press, 1978), p. 34.
2. C. Peter Wagner, *Your Spiritual Gifts Can Help Your Church Grow* (Ventura, CA: Regal Books, 1979).
3. C. Peter Wagner, "Evangelizing the Real America," *The Best in Theology*, Vol. 1 (Carol Stream, IL: Christianity Today, Inc., 1987), pp. 347-360.
4. David J. Hesselgrave, *Planting Churches Cross-Culturally: A Guide for Home and Foreign Missions* (Grand Rapids, MI: Baker Book House, 1980).
5. Jerry L. Appleby, *Missions Have Come Home to America* (Kansas City, MO: Beacon Hill Press, 1986).
6. Charles Brock, *The Principles and Practice of Indigenous Church Planting* (Nashville, TN: Broadman Press, 1981).
7. Bernard Quinn, et al., eds., *Churches and Church Membership in the United States 1980* (Atlanta, GA: Glenmary Research Center, 1982).
8. Ezra Earl Jones, *Strategies for New Churches* (New York, NY: Harper & Row, Publishers, 1976), p. 79.
9. Robert H. Schuller, *Your Church Has a Fantastic Future* (Ventura, CA: Regal Books, 1986), p. 246.

6

BUILDING THE NUCLEUS

The first step in actually planting the church, once the planning has been done and you know where you want the church to be located, is to begin to build the nucleus. Church planting expert, Robert E. Logan, likens church planting to human reproduction, calling the planning the "conception" and organizing the nucleus "prenatal development." The first public worship service is "birth."

Logan says, "If a church rushes into its first public worship service without having developed properly, it can suffer the same fate of a miscarried or aborted child. On the other hand, if a church spends too much time in prenatal development it will lose life-giving momentum and vision as a child loses life-giving blood and nutrients with the breakdown of the placenta."[1]

It takes nine months for a human baby to develop. Experience has shown that this might be a little too long for the nucleus building phase of a new church. If the proper planning is done and a competent feasibility study produced, it is well to plan for a nucleus building phase of four to six months. A longer period might have been called for in the past when we did not have today's know-how. But any church planter who is up-to-date on the field should have the techniques to make it happen in four to six months.

ATTRACTING NUCLEUS MEMBERS

Since a church is people, the first objective for a new church needs to be centered on people. This is why demographics—the study of populations—are so important in the planning phase. The initial group of people that you will need to work on is the nucleus. It is best not to call it a church at this point, even though in the strict sense of the word it is a church, just as a human fetus is a child.

I am going to list nine ways of attracting nucleus members. Not all nine may be useful to you. But some of them undoubtedly will be. I'm sure that there are other excellent methods that I have not included on my list, some of which probably have not yet been thought of and tested. Be flexible. If one method doesn't work, scrap it and try another. It is always well to keep in mind that developing a healthy nucleus is the goal, and methods used to accomplish the goal are secondary. Don't allow yourself to get hung up on a method as all too many church planters have done in the past.

1. *Hiving off.* If you have selected the model of hiving off a group of members from an existing church as your church planting methodology, you have the beginnings of a nucleus, or you may even have the entire nucleus needed. In the next chapter I will suggest some numbers for optimum nucleus size.

Some church planters prefer to recruit the nucleus and remain in the parent church during the four to six months of the nucleus building phase. Others prefer to move out and begin meeting separately as a nucleus in homes or other temporary facilities. A combination of both is most feasible for some.

The obvious advantages of developing the nucleus in the parent church are comfort, adequate facilities, child care, and a full-sized worship service. A disadvantage is that much energy, involuntary as it may be, is expended on the maintenance and the activities and the program of the parent church rather than focusing that energy on building the nucleus and leading up to the new church.

It takes nine months for a human baby to develop. Experience has shown that this might be a little too long for the nucleus building phase of a new church.

Another advantage has to do with social networks. One of the more difficult commitments that members of a hiving off nucleus make is that they will break off some longstanding social fellowship in order to make a new start in a new church. For many it is less painful to do this all at once rather than drawing out the process of separation over a longer period of time. I have also seen an extended period of time in the parent church measurably reduce the zeal and enthusiasm for planting a new church that the potential nucleus members felt when they accepted the challenge.

2. Home Bible studies. A very common way of building the nucleus is to organize one or more home Bible study groups that meet once a week, usually on a weeknight evening.

Keep in mind that the function of these particular Bible studies is to organize the nucleus for a new church. Some home Bible studies are organized primarily for Bible study, prayer, evangelism, fellowship or for pastoral care. All of these activities are good and necessary parts of church life, and all those ministries need to be taking place during the nucleus building phase and beyond. However, while all of the above might be included to some degree in the ministry of the home Bible studies, none is the primary goal. Building a nucleus is.

It is important to make each potential home Bible study member aware that if they decide to become a member of the group they should also be committed to be a part of the new church. While I realize that it may take some a few weeks to decide that God wants them with the new church, the possibility should at least be a viable option for them.

Distractions are many at this point. Some will begin attending because they like the teaching or because they have some close friends in the group or because they need some personal healing, but they have no intention of leaving their present church. Although it is very difficult for some church planters to do, these people should be weeded out and discouraged from attending the meetings. At this particular point in ministry, God has called you to build the nucleus for a new church, and you should invest all the time and energy available to you to accomplish the task. Be single-minded. Pour your life into those whom God is giving you for the new church, not into otherwise very worthy individuals who can sidetrack you.

It is even more difficult for some to resist the temptation to be diverted from church planting by evangelistic opportunities. While each home Bible study should be evangelistically sensitive and while outreach to the unchurched should begin aggressively at this stage, evangelistic efforts should be focused primarily on individuals and families who are both open to the gospel at this point in time and also open to being members of a new church. There are always many others who are not characterized by either of the above but who need Jesus Christ as Lord and Savior. Put their names on file, and reach out to them once the new church is operational.

Be single-minded. Pour your life into those whom God is giving you for the new church, not into otherwise worthy individuals who can sidetrack you.

---

3. Door-to-door. Field reports of the use of door-to-door methods for building a nucleus are spotty. For some it has worked wonderfully, for some it has flopped, and others are in between. Why? There are several variables that are known, and undoubtedly many others that are yet to be discovered. The personality of the individual who makes the call is a chief factor, as all door-to-door sales companies know. Another is the match of the person to the audience. I could imagine, for example, how much success I would have going door-to-door in Iran. Another is the social climate of the neighborhood itself. Some residents dislike strangers knocking at their door so much that they live in gated communities where everyone who enters the neighborhood is first screened by a security guard.

One of the more helpful suggestions for increasing the effectiveness of the door-to-door method is a concept from the real estate industry called "farming." This means that instead of trying to knock on every door of the city at least once, the efforts are concentrated in a more restricted area of the city where you can knock on the same door time after time. One church in San Jose, California, that tried farming for six months had 50 new families visit their church; seven families joined, and attendance soared.

Through repeated contact and little gifts left at each visit, the pastor becomes an acquaintance and then a friend to many. If they are not involved with a church, but something comes up where they feel they need a church, they know where to look. Attractive brochures describing the church are good things to leave. A real estate book I read also suggested: scratch pads, plastic coasters, pencils, pens, kites, shoe horns, pot holders, and back scratchers, all imprinted with the name, address and telephone number of the church. These can be obtained quite inexpensively and are a good investment from a part of the evangelism budget.

4. *Door-to-door prayer.* I first heard of using prayer for outreach as I was studying the "Rosario Plan" engineered by Edgardo Silvoso in Rosario, Argentina in 1976. A Nazarene Pastor, Bruno Radizeski, organized home prayer meetings in several neighborhoods of the city. He instructed his people to go door-to-door throughout the neighborhood 30 minutes before the prayer meeting, asking the families for requests that they could pray about later in the evening at So-and-So's house down the street. The next week they would visit the families to see how God had answered and collect more prayer requests. They found people much more open to receive this kind of ministry than they would be to an invitation to a church meeting or a presentation of the Four Spiritual Laws.

My friend Juan Agosto, who was pastoring a Hispanic church while taking a degree at Fuller Seminary, used this method to good effect. His church became a distributing center for surplus government cheese and honey. Neighborhood people who came to receive their allotment by regulation had to leave their name, address, telephone number and names of family members. On Wednesday nights before the weekly prayer meeting, Agosto sent out teams of two or three to the families who received food, and invited them to give prayer requests to the church that night. The church outgrew its building, and plans were made to move into a larger facility.

5. *Children's events.* Sponsoring children's events that are specifically designed to reach the parents have proved to be very effective in building the nucleus for a new church. I mentioned previously that the Southern Baptists have used college students on summer vacation to plant new churches. One of the principal methods is to hold daily vacation Bible schools in the neighborhoods. Many unchurched parents are glad for their children to have something organized to do for a couple of weeks, and since the Bible school is in their own neighborhood, they trust it. Of course the children receive great benefit themselves, some of them coming to know Jesus as their personal Savior. But more than that, since this is a nucleus building event, the closing exercises draw in the parents and they are usually open to subsequent visits and ministry. Some of them decide to become Christians and join the new church.

A friend of mine who started a new church in Colorado Springs used a relatively simple, but very effective technique for getting in personal touch with parents of younger children in his ministry area. He rented the gymnasium of the neighborhood elementary school for a Saturday and held a children's fair. He dressed it up with balloons and streamers and posters. He installed several carnival-like games, one of which was throwing a wet sponge to see if they could hit the pastor's face poked through a panel. Music and refreshments made it an exciting place for the children and their parents. Those were the days when E.T. was popular, so a volunteer was dressed up like E.T., and the children were invited to have a free picture taken with E.T. The parents left their names and addresses, and a week later the pastor visited them with the free picture. Friendly, personal contacts were abundant.

Special Events and Advertising

6. *Adult events.* Another good way to attract nucleus members is through special events designed to meet the needs of adults. In order to do this well you must first have a good idea as to what the felt needs of adults in your target audience might be. Your feasibility study will uncover many of these if it is well done. Even more important than that is to undertake a target audience opinion poll, which I will describe in detail in a subsequent chapter.

My friend, Mark Platt, who supervises church planting for the Conservative Baptists of Northern California, frequently targets baby boomers as potential nucleus members. In his area divorce rates are very high and young people want to develop marriages that will be more permanent and fulfilling. So Platt, knowing about this felt need, holds a series of marriage seminars on weeknights in order to contact adults for the nucleus of the new church.

I first met John Wimber when he was a Quaker pastor in the mid-seventies. He told me that he had done a survey of young married families in his ministry area and found that the number one felt need of young mothers was potty training. So he hired a child psychologist who was an expert in potty training and sponsored a seminar. He tacked up flyers on the bulletin boards of laundromats and grocery stores and distributed them at shopping centers. Many came, paid their $5.00 and filled out the registration card with their name and address. Wimber's evangelistic teams went out to call on them afterward, and several new families came into the churches as a result. As Robert Schuller says, "The secret of success is to find a need and fill it."

7. *Church planting crusades.* It is difficult for most of us to relate crusade evangelism to church planting because the models we have become accustomed to do not emphasize multiplying churches. In recent years, however, crusades have been used for church planting with good success.

My friend Edgardo Silvoso of Harvest Evangelism is one of the pioneers of this kind of ministry conducted according to the traditional interdenominational format. The big difference is that the central thrust of his city-wide evangelistic effort is planting churches. The bulk of the precrusade training and preparation is to develop nuclei for new churches throughout the city. Then when the new converts come, they are funnelled into the nuclei, which in turn become new churches. He did this some years ago in Rosario, Argentina, and his most recent crusade is centered on the city of Resistencia, Argentina, where Silvoso hopes to see 400 new churches established.

More frequently, crusades have been used to plant one local church, rather than many churches interdenominationally. Seventh-Day Adventists have been doing it for years. Many Pentecostals and others use this method. They typically put up a tent near the future site of the church and have nightly evangelistic meetings for weeks or months at a time. Special meetings are then organized at different times for nurturing the converts and assimilating them into the nucleus of the new church. Missionary-evangelist David Goodwin with the Assemblies of God has an excellent book on church planting crusades, *Church Planting Methods.*[2]

8. *Advertising.* Advertising, like door-to-door, brings different responses from the field. One pastor will tell me, "We spent a fortune on advertising and got virtually nothing back." Another, like Rick Warren, will tell me that up to half of the new people who come to their church are initially drawn through advertising. What is the difference? If I do not miss my guess, the primary variable is professionalism. Advertising has become such a sophisticated industry that amateur attempts have little chance of anything but failure.

Three general forms of commercial-level advertising have been used for nucleus building: space advertising, direct-mail, and telemarketing. I am going to deal with telemarketing under a separate category, so let's look at the other two.

I honestly do not have much data on the effectiveness of space advertising. Studies have shown that a church's advertisement on Saturday's religious page has usually functioned more as a morale builder for church members rather than as an attraction for the unchurched. Unless there is some featured special event, space ads serve mostly as image builders, the results of which are very difficult to measure. If you do use space advertising for the unchurched, be sure you have the best of professional expertise and keep it off the Saturday religion page.

The Christian and Missionary Alliance (C&MA) set what I believe to be a national record on Easter Sunday 1987 by planting 101 churches that single day. The largest was in Kaiser, Oregon, with 302 people and the smallest in Blackfoot, Idaho, with 21. In Nampa, Idaho, they saw 50 conversions the first two Sundays. These churches were mostly started through direct mail advertising. The average budget for building each nucleus was around $10,000, which covered the pastor's salary for three months, plus postage to mail 30,000 hand-addressed letters, focusing on the needs of the target audience that had been previously determined by a community survey. The C&MA leaders estimate that over 80 percent of those who came to the churches on the first Sunday were unchurched.

It is important that your mailings say the right things and are sent to the right people. Here is where the services of a company like Church Information and Development Services (CIDS) can help enormously. Once you know which of the 50 life-style segments compose your target audience, CIDS can help you put together a direct mail program based on an analysis of the Micro-Vision Segments, which will assure you that your mailing will go primarily to those census tracts or zip codes that have high concentrations of people who belong to your target audience.

Another way you can advertise by direct mail is to get in touch with Gospel Publishing Association (Box 94638, Birmingham, Alabama 35220, 205-681-1339), and ask them for information on the custom-made tabloid that they will mail out for your church. For a reasonable fee, they will mail an attractive eight-page newspaper once a month for nine months, with about 30 percent of the space in each issue available for your own church advertising. The rest is filled with plain vanilla, family-oriented Christian articles.

And Finally...the Telephone
9. *Telemarketing.* For reasons that I can easily understand, mention telemarketing for planting a new church to a group of pastors and you get nothing but a loud groan. Some polls have shown that the number one nuisance for many Americans is junk telephone calls. I for one would vote that way. However, when you think about it, there must be a reason that those calls keep coming—somehow they must work!

Norm Whan of Church Growth Development International has known this for a long time. When he gave his life to Jesus Christ not too many years ago, he asked God to show him how his professional expertise could be used for the kingdom of God. God led him to adapt his telemarketing skills to church planting. I was as skeptical as anyone when he told me in 1985 that he was planning to start a church by using the telephone. A few months later Mountain View Friends Church, his pilot project, was off and running with 261 attending the first service. Since then Whan's *The Phone's for You!*[3] resource has been used to plant some 2,500 new churches across regional and denominational boundaries, some internationally. As an example, in a six-week period in the spring of 1989, the Presbyterian Church of America alone started churches in Milwaukee (140 the first Sunday), Birmingham (181), Sacramento (270). Jacksonville (242), Las Vegas (280), and San Diego (338), all through telemarketing. In most cases, with eight weeks of effort, you will be ready to launch your first worship service with 150 to 200 people in attendance. Typically, the second Sunday will be about half of the first in attendance. This then becomes the nucleus from which you build your church.

This is an outworking of what Whan calls "the law of large numbers." It is highly predictable that 20,000 dial ups will produce 2,000 names for the mailing list, and 200 of them will come to the first service. Once a name goes on the mailing list, they receive a series of five direct mail pieces in preparation for the first service. In a *Time* magazine article (headline: "Many Are Called ") Whan is quoted as saying, "Most ministries realize how to reach rural people, but there are millions in cities; in high rises and behind gates."[4] While telemarketing won't reach them all, it can reach many who otherwise might not hear the message of salvation.

As your nucleus of new church members grows and develops, more and more of your vision, energy and activity become focused on the purpose of all this prenatal development. Like an expectant parent, excitement builds as you approach the moment of anticipation: the birth of your new church in its first public worship service.

NOTES
1. Robert E. Logan, *Starting a Church that Keeps on Growing* (The Charles E. Fuller Institute for Evangelism and Church Growth, Box 91990, Pasadena, CA 91109, 800-999-9578, 1986), p. 8. Robert Logan's church planting resources, published by the Charles E. Fuller Institute, are in my opinion the finest trans-denominational resources available. His *Church Planting Workbook*, co-authored with Jeff Rast, is the most valuable tool you can have if you are actually planting a new church. The *Church Planter's Checklist* is a companion resource. On an executive level, Logan and Rast have also written *A Supervisor's Manual for New Church Development*.
2. David E. Goodwin, *Church Planting Methods: A "How-To" Book of Overseas Church Planting Crusades* (DeSoto, TX: Lifeshare Communications, 1984).
3. Norm Whan, *The Phone's for You!* available from Church Growth Development International, 420 W. Lambert, Suite E, Brea, CA 92621 (714-990-9551).
4. Richard K. Ostling, "Many Are Called," *Time*, February 24, 1989.

7

GOING PUBLIC

No single day from the time the idea for a new church is first generated until it becomes an established church is more crucial than the day the new church goes public. This is the same with a human baby, and it is the chief reason the birthday is celebrated each year throughout the person's lifetime.

Presumably you have a nucleus that is prepared to take the leap and become a church. Before it does, be as confident as possible that the three items on this checklist have been adequately cared for: the spiritual dynamic, the philosophy of ministry and the lay leadership.

THE SPIRITUAL DYNAMIC

It is time to remind ourselves once again that church planting is a spiritual enterprise. The real battle is not fought with demographic reports, feasibility studies, evangelistic methodologies, purchase of real estate or raising funds. The real battle is a spiritual one in which Satan will do all he can to prevent the new church from starting or see that it is a crippled one if it does. This is why it is so important for the spiritual tone to be at its peak when it comes time to go public.

One of the most amazing things to me is that human beings reject God's love. If people understood the magnitude of the deal God is offering them free of charge, no one in their right mind could possibly refuse it. One of the problems is that they don't really understand how much God loves them and what He has done for them through the Cross. A chief task of Satan is to put a veil over the gospel so that unbelievers cannot understand it. In 2 Corinthians 4:3,4 the apostle Paul says that the gospel is veiled to those who are perishing because "the god of this age has blinded the minds of unbelievers, so that they cannot see the light of the gospel of the glory of Christ, who is the image of God." Our weapons for dealing with this veil of unbelief are essentially spiritual, not carnal.

Love
There are several dimensions to the spiritual tone of the nucleus that is soon to become a church. One of them is love. Love is the supreme fruit of the Holy Spirit. Loving God is the starting point, but here I am referring mainly to the members of the nucleus loving one another and showing that love by their deeds.

Fellowship is crucial for love to develop. The people need to spend much time together in situations where they can be relaxed and open with each other. There are many ways this can be accomplished, such as home cell groups, adult Sunday School classes, church suppers, minidinners bringing together three or four couples in a home for a potluck, ministry teams, retreats and other activities. But the key to making it happen is time. Nothing establishes fellowship like time spent together.

There is a danger here. The fellowship can get so intense that it becomes an end in itself. *Koinonia* can become "koinonitis," as I point out in my book *Your Church Can Be Healthy.*[1] The last thing you want on the day you go public is a nucleus with a case of koinonitis. Visitors will spot the symptoms a mile away and feel that they are not really welcome. For this reason, love for the lost must be a high value, high enough to put aside some of the warm fuzzy feelings of intimacy in the nucleus in order to embrace the newcomers when the church goes public.

Faith

Faith is another fruit of the Spirit and an extremely important spiritual characteristic for the nucleus to exhibit. Volunteering to be part of a new church start is in itself an act of faith, so we can safely presume that the nucleus members will have a higher than average level of faith to begin with. But this is only a starting point. Those with some faith can develop more with the help of God, and with coaching from the leader.

Faith, according to Hebrews 11:1, is the substance of things hoped for. The nucleus should be looking to the future, seeing what God wants the new church to be, and putting substance on that vision. They should believe with all their heart that God is going to use them to do a great work in the target community. They should know that God wants them to move forward and that the very gates of Hell cannot prevent that new church from being planted.

In the nucleus building phase they should have learned to exercise faith in financial matters. I have not said much about money up to this point, but the subject cannot be ignored. Many of the nucleus members may already have known what it is to tithe and to continue giving far beyond the tithe. They should set the example for the others. Biblical patterns of giving should be well in place before going public because the first few worship services are not the time to talk much about money. If any of the nucleus members are not tithing to the church, I would let them know that it is a serious problem. It is serious because it may indicate that their heart is not really in starting a new church. Jesus says, "Where your treasure is, there your heart will be also" (Matt. 6:21).

You should reduce your philosophy of ministry to a catchy slogan that everybody in the church can memorize easily and communicate with others.

I also suggest that the nucleus members form the habit of caring for the financial needs of other nucleus members as they arise. A sensitive screening process needs to be in place, but when it is, there is nothing more satisfying to a group of believers than to know each other's financial needs and to give generously to help meet them. It is a supreme manifestation of a combination of love and faith. Others will notice it after the church goes public.

Prayer
I know I have mentioned prayer previously, but the older I get and the more I learn about God, the more I realize that we can hardly say too much about it. Prayer, along with the Word of God, is our chief spiritual weapon. "The prayer of a righteous man is powerful and effective" (Jas. 5:16). Much

prayer and prayer life emerges spontaneously from the heart, but not all. Prayer is also a learned behavior pattern that can both be caught and taught. I would not want to launch out and go public with a nucleus that was not an enthusiastic and practicing group of pray-ers. The leaders especially should be modeling their priority commitment to prayer in all aspects.

THE PHILOSOPHY OF MINISTRY

The second item on the checklist for going public is the philosophy of ministry for the new church. I listed philosophy of ministry as one of the basic essentials for planning in chapter 3, but I did not go into much detail. You need the first pass at a philosophy of ministry to set the direction even before starting to build the nucleus, but ordinarily during the nucleus building phase you will have discovered many additional areas where your original philosophy of ministry needs some revision. The best time to update it is shortly before you go public.

As I have said, the philosophy of ministry addresses two principal questions: who? and how? The question of whom God has called us and equipped us to reach should be fairly well answered as you are coming to the end of the nucleus building stage and getting ready to go public. The visitors who attend your first worship services will be more likely to consider coming back again if they see people around them with whom they feel comfortable. This is a human characteristic with which we may not agree, but that we must recognize if we intend to meet and minister to people where they are rather than where we might want them to be some day.

The second question: How are we going to reach them? may not be as clear when you first go public as it will be a year hence. Settling down to effective methods requires much trial and error. Nevertheless it is well to take all the time and energy necessary to refine and establish your philosophy of ministry at this point. Here are five characteristics of a good philosophy of ministry to keep in mind:

1. *The philosophy of ministry is explicit.* Get your philosophy of ministry in writing. It is well to write it on three levels. For one thing, you should have a detailed document of several pages that deals with things like your leadership style, your expectation from the church members, your charismatic position, your ethical stands, your worship style, your musical program, your statement of faith, your fellowship groups, your budget process, and whatever else you consider important. For another, this should be condensed in the form of a brief, readable brochure that you pass out to all visitors. Finally, you should reduce it to a catchy slogan that everybody in the church can memorize easily and communicate with others.

2. *The philosophy of ministry is mutual.* The primary generating source for the philosophy of ministry should be the leading of the Holy Spirit through the person of the church planter. But a wise church planter will consult widely with the opinion makers in the nucleus before writing the philosophy of ministry. This will help assure mutual agreement between the pastor and the people. Numerous churches are hobbling along in a survival mode because the people assume one philosophy of ministry and the pastor assumes another.

3. *The philosophy of ministry needs to be a conviction.* No one should doubt that the reason why we do things this way is because that is the way God wants us to do them. In dynamic churches the people are convinced that theirs is the most biblical philosophy of ministry of all.

This is not usually an expression of spiritual pride, but of a deep commitment to Jesus Christ.

4. The philosophy of ministry needs to be stable. Changes in the philosophy of ministry, particularly substantial changes, greatly weaken a church. But this must be balanced by the last characteristic:

5. The philosophy of ministry needs to be open to modification. As times and circumstances change, the philosophy of ministry must change with them. Be open to this, but be sure that God is the one who is leading you to change it.

LAY LEADERSHIP

The third item on the checklist for going public is lay leadership. By leadership I do not mean leading the church as a whole. This is the responsibility of the church planter and the pastor. I mean leadership in the various areas of ministry. In the healthiest of churches, the pastor is doing the leading while the lay people are doing the ministry.

I believe that the best way to introduce lay people to ministry is to help them discover, develop and use their spiritual gifts. This takes teaching, modeling and practice. The Charles E. Fuller Institute has made available a set of high-quality resources to aid you in the process of helping people to know which gifts God has given them and to place them in church ministries which will be challenging and fulfilling to them.[2]

I myself have attempted to do this through the years in my Sunday School class at Lake Avenue Congregational Church called the 120 Fellowship. I am in charge of the spiritual development and ministry of about 100 adults, a group larger than the average U.S. church. About 80 percent of the class members know their spiritual gifts and are using them in ministry. I have seven ministry teams, all under competent lay leadership: Administration, Pastoral Care, Healing Prayer, Worship, Intercession, Outreach and Widows Indeed. I am proud of the team leaders and those who minister on each team, and I know you will be, too, as your people discover their spiritual gifts. The more ministry teams you have in place before you go public, the smoother will be the transition from a nucleus to a church.

THE NAME

Presumably up to now you have not been calling your nucleus a "church." It is advisable to reserve this term for the day you go public. If in the nucleus building phase you invite an unchurched person to come to visit your "church" and they find out there may be 20 or 25 people there, they may turn down that invitation simply because they think there must be something wrong if a church is only that size. But inviting them to a "Bible study" will help neutralize that objection.

Think twice before using the name of your denomination or the city in which you plant the church. Not that these names should never be used, but ask yourself what they mean to the *unchurched* public. Robert Schuller did not call what was originally the Garden Grove Community Church a "Reformed" church, even though he was sent out to plant a Reformed Church of America congregation. He had found that the unchurched associated "reformed church" with "reform school," and they didn't want to be a part of that. An Evangelical Covenant pastor discovered that people in his community were reading "covenant" as "convent." Rick Warren knew that the name Southern Baptist carried a negative image for many in California. So Rick, a thoroughly committed Southern Baptist, called his church the Saddleback Valley Community Church. Since then, over 50 other California Southern Baptist churches have dropped the denominational label or started without it. Warren says that he would put Baptist in capital letters if he were planting a church in North Carolina. It's OK to use the denominational name provided you think it through first.

Schuller found he had made a slight mistake in using "Garden Grove" in the name. It didn't hurt the growth much, but as soon as he had a good reason to, he changed the name to Crystal Cathedral. He found that his ministry area was ever so much broader than the city of Garden Grove. Rick Warren wisely did not attach "Laguna Hills" to his church name even though that was their first location. Since then they have changed locations to Mission Viejo, and now they have purchased property in El Toro. All of those communities are in the Saddleback Valley.

Do not shy away from the name "church." There was a time back in the 1960s and 1970s when segments of the American population spoke out against the church, and some churches decided to call themselves centers or fellowships or chapels or communities. But each year the Gallup poll asks Americans their opinions about their confidence in American institutions, and the church usually comes out at the top of the list. Americans in general are attracted, not repelled, by the name "church."

The Critical Mass

In nuclear physics the critical mass is the minimum amount of fissionable material necessary to produce a chain reaction. In church planting it indicates the size a viable nucleus needs to be at the time of going public, if the church is to grow well.

If the long-range plan for the church is to be under 200, the critical mass can be as small as 25 or 30 adults. However, if the plan is for the church to grow to over 200 that is too small. The critical mass should be between 50 and 100 adults. There may well be many variables that determine ideal nucleus size, but I am so far aware of only one study. It suggests that for a blue-collar, working-class church you can start near the lower end of the range, but for a professional, white-collar church you do better toward the top part of the range.

Research by the Southern Baptist Home Mission Board has shown that Southern Baptist churches going public with under 50 have three times the rate of failure as those that start with over 50. It wouldn't surprise me if this applied to most other denominations as well.

The Meeting Place

As I will explain more fully in the next chapter, I recommend that the first meeting place for the new church be leased or rented property, not in a church building that has been constructed for the purpose. Mark Platt recommends that his Conservative Baptist church planters investigate the following as possibilities: restaurants, YMCAs, YWCAs, public or private schools, skating rinks, mortuaries, community centers, bank or motel conference rooms, Seventh Day Adventist churches, Jewish synagogues, or other church buildings at alternate times. He says, "There is great wisdom in delaying the purchase and development of property so that the new church can put its best efforts ministering to people."[3] I agree.

The feasibility of one rented facility or another will differ greatly according to the local circumstances and what kind of a church is projected. However, I feel that one greatly underutilized space in many of our communities are hotel or motel conference rooms. These are often full during the week, but empty on weekends. Hotel sales managers would like to keep them full seven days a week. The prices on these rooms are in most cases highly negotiable. During the week they are free of charge if you book enough of the hotel rooms for conference participants. Could it be that on Sunday they could be discounted or even free if enough

---

The idea of "house churches" was advocated in the 1960s and widely experimented with in the 1970s, and the evidence is now in: they did not work well.

---

church members agreed to have Sunday brunch in the hotel restaurant on a regular basis?

Keep in mind that hotel or motel conference rooms are equipped with climate control, flexible partitions, movable seating, lighting, carpeted floors, platforms, audio equipment and janitorial service. Breakout rooms may be available for Sunday School classes or nurseries. Most have high visibility and accessibility. Using these facilities does require weekly set up and take down, but think of that as an excellent opportunity for ministry for some individuals who will never be pastors or Sunday School teachers or trustees or evangelists, but who want to serve the Lord with the skills they do have.

The one place I would not advise that you use for going public is a residence. In almost every case it will greatly reduce your growth potential. By this I do not mean a residence that is being totally used as a church facility but one in which people currently live. The idea of "house church-es" was advocated in the 1960s and widely experimented with in the 1970s, and the evidence is now in: they did not work well.

Announcing the Event

Get as much professional help as you possibly can for announcing the first public worship service of your church to the general public in your target community. Space advertising and direct mail have proved very useful. In the direct mail, some have used a "birth announcement" theme to good advantage. Radio spots can help. Notices and flyers in public areas like shopping centers can also attract some.

Plan your birth date carefully. Times to avoid include Super Bowl Sunday, the two Sundays of changing to and from daylight saving time, and December through early January. With the possible exception of the summer months or the months of extreme cold and snow in the frost belt, most any other time will do. There is some consensus that, other things being equal, Easter Sunday may be the best starting date of all.

The First Worship Service

The chief commodity you have to offer to nonnucleus members who respond to your invitations and show up on the day you go public is your worship service. Spare no effort in planning it well. Several church planters I know have held dress rehearsals of the worship service with nucleus members, practicing the sermon and all. My friend David Arp of Anchorage, Alaska, practiced his worship service for four Sundays, and later said that he needed them all to work out the kinks. Rick Warren held his rehearsal on Palm Sunday, intending to go public on Easter, but some unchurched people got their dates confused and showed up. Six were saved!

Be sure that the worship service and all other activities that day are focused on the visitors. This is no time for nucleus members who have grown to love each other over the past weeks and months to slap each other on the back and enjoy a mutual congratulations party. Save that until later. Visitors deserve all the attention you can possibly give them especially throughout the first few weeks.

Experience has shown that there are three crucial things that will impress visitors who decide to try the church out: (1) Is the sermon interesting and does it apply to my life? (2) Is the child care up to par? The first question young parents ask their children when they take them out of the nursery or Sunday School is, "Did you have a good time?" As much as anything else, the answer to that question will determine whether they return. (3) Does the church want my money? This is the reason why I mentioned that it is not advisable to put much stress on money during the first few weeks after going public.

Other things such as personal greetings, comfortable seating, the music program, and coffee and doughnuts are important as well, but not as important as the three crucial questions.

Independence

Some new churches start on their own, but others are dependent in the beginning on support from another church or a church planting agency. If the new church is dependent, it is well to agree from the start how long this dependence will last. A survey made by *Leadership* magazine found that the average time was 12 months, after which the new church should be on its own with finances, personnel and program.

When is a new church no longer a "new church?" I believe that a new church can and will sustain the vigor of youth so long as it has unmet growth goals and it is moving toward them. The Garden Grove Community Church (now Crystal Cathedral) maintained its atmosphere of newness for about 20 years, a remarkably long time. Most churches lose it when they plateau in their growth for a period of time or when the first permanent pastor leaves and a new one comes in. My recommendation is to keep setting goals, keep your growth momentum, and stay new as long as possible. The next chapter gives some ways and means of making that happen.

NOTES
1. C. Peter Wagner, *Your Church Can Be Healthy* (Nashville, TN: Abingdon, 1979).
2. Resources on spiritual gifts available through the Charles E. Fuller Institute, Box 91990, Pasadena, CA 91109-1990 (800-999-9578) include:
    a. C. Peter Wagner. *Your Spiritual Gifts Can Help Your Church Grow.* Ventura, CA: Regal Books, 1979. The basic text for pastors and lay people.
    b. C. Peter Wagner. *Spiritual Gifts Workshop.* A do-it-yourself six-hour workshop to be led by the pastor. This contains Wagner's complete lecture on spiritual gifts for the pastor to listen to before conducting the workshop.
    c. C. Peter Wagner. *Video Spiritual Gifts Workshop.* Wagner himself conducts the spiritual gifts workshop on video.
    d. *Wagner Modified Houts Questionnaire.* This is the most popular gifts inventory currently available. It tests for 25 gifts, including the sign gifts. Other instruments without the sign gifts include the original *Houts Inventory of Spiritual Gifts,* the *Wesley Spiritual Gifts Questionnaire,* and the *Trenton Spiritual Gifts Analysis.*
    e. Robert E. Logan and Janet Logan. *Spiritual Gifts Implementation.* This self-study kit with a video tape and a workbook picks up where Wagner leaves off. Wagner helps people discover their gifts, the Logans help them put these gifts to use in local church ministry.
    f. Bruce L. Bugbee. *Networking.* The way it is done in the well-known Willow Creek Community Church.
3. Mark Platt, "Church Obstetrics: How a Church Is Born," pamphlet published by Conservative Baptist Association of Northern California, 18510 Prospect

8

WILL YOUR NEW CHURCH GROW?

The time to begin planning for the growth of the new church is at the very beginning. Research has shown that setting specific goals for a church releases growth dynamics that otherwise would remain bottled up. No less a church growth practitioner than Paul Yonggi Cho says, "The number one requirement for having real church growth—unlimited church growth—is to set goals."[1] A reason why goal setting taps into a source of spiritual power is that it reflects faith. I agree with Ed Dayton who says, "Every goal is a statement of faith."

One of the things that impressed me about Rick Warren when I first came across him in 1980 was his unusual aptitude for goal setting. Before he began building the nucleus for Saddleback Community Church he publicly announced that his goal was 20,000 members by the year 2020. He also announced that he hoped to start one new church a year during those 40 years. His first decade is coming to a close. He is right on the curve toward the 20,000 and has planted 14 new churches so far instead of 10.

I'm not saying that simply by setting goals you will have a church like Cho's or Warren's. They obviously have other things going for them as well. But I am saying that if you take goal setting seriously you will in all probability end up with a church considerably larger than you would have without doing it.

HOW LARGE SHOULD MY CHURCH BE?

The most important decision to make concerning the future size of the new church is whether you feel God wants it to be under 200 or over 200. Your guiding principle for any planning in Christian work is, of course, the will of God. I believe God desires multitudes of churches that will never have more than 200 members. I believe He also desires multitudes of churches that will be over 200. He therefore calls and equips pastoral leaders for both types of ministry. One of the most important things church planters can do is to come to terms with God's desire for their own personal ministry. If they could it would avoid a great deal of unnecessary grief and frustration.

Let me explain the number 200. For years church leaders had noticed that new churches tend to grow up to around 200, then plateau off with ups and downs almost indefinitely. A considerable amount of research has now been done on this "200 barrier," and the dynamics of why it is there and how it can be avoided are fairly well understood.

Take note that the 200 represents active adults in your congregation. By active I do not necessarily mean that they attend 52 Sundays a year and give $8,000 a year in offerings. But they do attend and they do give, and you mutually recognize that your church is their church and that you are their pastor. Furthermore, the 200 is not a fixed number, but the median point in a range between 150 and 250. Depending on growth dynamics, some churches hit the barrier at the low point of 150, while others will not stall out until they approach 250. You should not rest assured that you are over the 200 barrier until you have at least 350 active adults.

Churches under 200 have their strengths. They meet people's needs. Large numbers of unbelievers who couldn't be won to Christ in large churches can be won in small churches. If God lets you know that He wants you to pastor a small church, don't regard it as a put-down. Regard it as a privileged order from the Master. Carl Dudley points out that members of a small church have a high degree of satisfaction with their situation. "The small church is already the right size," says Dudley, "for everyone to know, or know about, everyone else....The essential character of the small church is this capacity to care about people personally."[2]

If God intends for your church to be small, you can have a healthy church without a great deal of extra effort. If you have done a good feasibility study and are located in the right place, if you have built a viable nucleus, and you have a reasonably strong evangelistic zeal to see new people won to Christ and drawn into the church, you can expect a comfortable, family-style church of between 100 and 200 adults. However, if God indicates that He wants you to lead your church past 200, there is some specific action that you need to take.

Six Ways to Break the 200 Barrier
It is much easier never to stop at the 200 barrier than it is to turn a church around that has plateaued under 200. It is much more preferable to sustain growth momentum than to lose it and then attempt to regain it. That is why I recom-

mend that you make your decision as to size early in the process and from the very beginning build in safeguards to avoid stalling out.

As a part of some research she was doing, my wife, Doris, once asked Bill M. Sullivan, author of *Ten Steps to Breaking the Two Hundred Barrier* [3]: "In a brief statement, how do we tell pastors to break the 200 barrier?" Bill answered in one word: "Quickly!" What was he saying? He

---

To the greatest extent possible build your staff gift by gift so you can cover the broadest spectrum of ministry with the maximum competence.

---

was saying that the new church, even though it may have only 75 members, should never be a small church. It should never be allowed to become a single cell. Actually, if you understand church growth principles and have followed the recommendations in this book, you should expect to pass through the 200 barrier within about twelve months after going public. If you are not through it in two years, something is going wrong and your chances of ever doing it are greatly diminished. Perhaps God, after all, does want your church to be a small one.

Church growth is a combination of so many institutional, contextual and spiritual factors that I cannot guarantee you will pass through the 200 barrier. But I can say that your chances of doing so will be excellent if you follow as many of these six principles as possible.

1. *Staffing.* If at all possible, begin the new church with two staff members. I am referring to program staff, not backup staff such as secretaries, accountants and custodians. I am aware that this is impossible in many cases and if it is impossible, then start with one, but plan to add the second before you get to 100 active adults, the third before you get to 200, and so on until you have 500 and are safely past the 200 barrier. I realize that this sounds like too much staff at first, but the reason for this is that most of us have been mentally programmed with staff ratios designed for maintenance, not for growth. What I am suggesting is a growth ratio.

Many ask who the second staff member should be, or the third. They usually expect me to suggest a pastor of evangelism or music or youth or what have you. But I believe that there are certain basic principles or indicators that should underlie staff selection. The three primary factors in selecting a new staff member are: (1) Prior agreement with the philosophy of ministry. It is risky to hire people on staff with the idea that you will later indoctrinate them into your philosophy of ministry. If at all possible make sure they heartily agree with it beforehand. (2) Bringing spiritual gifts to the staff that are not already there and that will contribute to the implementation of the philosophy of ministry. If all the staff have the same spiritual gifts, you are headed for a deep rut. To the greatest extent possible build your staff gift by gift so you can cover the broadest spectrum of ministry with the maximum competence. (3) Loyalty. Total loyalty of every staff member to the senior pastor is a must for a healthy growth dynamic.

Where do you find your additional staff members? The traditional sources of seminary graduates and staffs of other churches are good. In addition to that a new trend has arisen through churches of several denominations to seek to recruit new staff from the members of the congregation. When lay leaders in the congregation are elevated to staff level, the three considerations of philosophy of ministry, giftedness, and loyalty are almost automatically built into the selection process. In most cases this will imply challenging believers to make a mid-career change from secular work to full-time ministry. To accommodate this, nontraditional methodologies of training workers are being developed, bypassing residential seminary and Bible school programs.

2. Fellowship groups. The major difference between a church under the 200 barrier and one over the 200 barrier is fellowship groups. The typical church under 200 is one single fellowship group, called by experts such as Carl Dudley and Lyle Schaller a "single cell church." Schaller says, "The strong commitment of the members to one another, to kinfolk ties, to the meeting place, to the concept that the congregation should function as one big family, and the modest emphasis on program tend to reinforce the single cell character of the small church."[4] This means very simply that if a new church is to go through the 200 barrier it should never be allowed to become a single cell church.

The best way to avoid this is to provide from day one, multiple options for adult fellowship groups. These fellowship groups can take the forms of cell groups of 8 to 12 persons each or congregations of 35 to 80 each or ministry teams or combinations of them. They can be special interest groups, task-oriented groups, or simply groups to provide koinonia and mutual care.[5]

The organization of multiple fellowship groups should begin during the building of the nucleus. Seeing that this happens is not easy. It can range from difficult to traumatic. People generally do not want to be told that they must distance themselves from others whom they have come to love and with whom they feel comfortable. The natural, almost inexorable tendency is for the nucleus to become a single cell, one happy fellowship group. Even nucleus members who from the beginning have understood this and have agreed not to let it happen will frequently find themselves involuntarily clinging to the security of their fellowship group and resisting—with considerable emotion—the admonitions of the pastor to form new groups.

Sometimes the church planters themselves will succumb to the pressure and find themselves unable to cause the formation of several groups or to sustain them once they are formed. Many don't even know it is happening and some time later ask themselves why they never got through the 200 barrier.

The group dynamic theory that underlies this is the rule of 40. Forty people is the ideal size for everyone to maintain a face-to-face relationship with everyone else. In a church setting the group can expand to 80 and sustain most of the interpersonal qualities. However, when it goes past 80 toward 200 the relationships are increasingly strained. By the time it gets to 150 most groups are so stressed out that they can no longer handle the thought of strangers entering the group and thereby increasing the stress. Without knowing they are doing it or without even wanting to, they relate to strangers like two identical poles of magnets.

Leading and Equipping

3. Leadership mode: Equipper. My suggestion is that the church planting pastor begin the new church as an equipper, not an enabler. In my book *Leading Your Church to Growth*, I define an equipper as "A leader who actively sets goals for a congregation according to the will of God, obtains goal ownership from the people, and sees that each church member is properly motivated and equipped to do his or her part in accomplishing the goals."[6]

There are two things that a pastor who intends to lead the church through the 200 barrier cannot delegate: leadership and vision. If you are a true leader, you cannot ask someone else to do your leading or even part of your leading for you. Experiments with copastors have failed at a rate I would guess to be ten to one. Unfortunately, our seminaries do not do a very good job in teaching leadership and as a result large numbers of practicing pastors are not the de facto leaders of their churches. As Lyle Schaller would say, they are hired by the church to be "medicine men" but not "tribal chiefs." They are expected to carry out the religious duties, but someone else leads the church. This is a major reason why many churches are not growing.

Elmer Towns says to his church planters: "The secret that will make your church different and successful from other fundamental churches in your area is leadership. 'Everything rises or falls on leadership.' Committee-run churches (those controlled by the deacons) rarely experience the growth of pastor-led churches."[7] This is what I have found as well.

Please do not think that I am advocating autocratic leadership or a dictatorial style. No. I am talking about God-anointed, spiritually gifted, servant leadership. According to the Bible, that is the only kind of leadership God blesses in the Church. Servanthood does not imply weakness as a leader. Leaders whom God uses for church growth are both humble and powerful. They are both servants and strong leaders. Biblically, leadership is not either-or but both-and.

The pastor who is an equipper is supremely dedicated to seeing that the lay people in the church are equipped for ministry. This usually implies helping them to recognize the spiritual gifts and natural talents that God has chosen to give them, then doing what is necessary to see that each one is able to use his or her gifts for the ministry of the body. The underlying motivation for this is not to recruit volunteers in order to get church tasks done, but to help each believer be all that God wants them to be.

It is good to let new people know right up front that if they want to become a part of your church body they will be expected to take part in ministry of one kind or another. My church, Lake Avenue Congregational Church, requires all new members to agree with "seven expectations" of membership. In the welcome brochure that visitors receive the first day they come to the church they are told that joining the church will imply their willingness to "use my spiritual gift(s) to minister to others in the church and in the world." If they do not yet know their spiritual gifts they can still join, but immediately afterward they take a three-session short course in gift discovery, after which they are funneled into a lay ministry placement process. If they don't want to use their spiritual gifts to minister, the implication is that they might be happier in some other church.

The best possible combination for growth occurs when the pastor concentrates on leading and equipping and the people concentrate on ministering. I believe that is what Ephesians 4:12 means when it describes the role of leaders "to prepare God's people for works of service."

4. *Pastoral Function: Rancher.* From the time you start building the nucleus mutually agree with the people that your pastoral function will be that of a rancher rather than a shepherd. In the shepherd mode the pastor is expected to know all of the people by name, know something about their family and their jobs, visit them occasionally, help them work out their personal problems, and maintain a type of family relationship with them. This can function well up to the 200 barrier, but not above it. Pastors whose job satisfaction depends heavily on a shepherding ministry are typically small church pastors.

A rancher mode can take the church through the 200 barrier. The essential difference between the shepherd and the rancher is not whether the sheep are cared for—they are in both cases if things are going as they should. The difference is who takes care of the sheep. The shepherd must do it personally, the rancher delegates the pastoral care to others. For example, my church has delegated to me the pastoral care of my Sunday School class, the 120 Fellowship. Even though I have only 100 adults, which is the size of a small church, I must function as a rancher, not a shepherd. So in order to do this, I have appointed a pastoral care team of 12 lay people. They were appointed because they had demonstrated that God had given them the spiritual gift of pastor and had been so recognized by the others. My people receive high-quality pastoral care, but not directly from me. There are three prominent symbols of the shepherd mode: home visitation, hospital visitation, and personal counseling, all of which I assiduously avoid. My people do not expect any of that from me, but they still love me. They love me because they know I am ultimately responsible for seeing they get the excellent care that they are receiving.

One of the most common reasons why pastors cannot be ranchers is that their people won't let them. This is particularly true in existing churches where all previous pastors have been shepherds. It is virtually impossible to be a rancher in churches like that because the people feel they are paying you a salary to give them personal attention. But this need not be the case in a new church, and that is one of the reasons why I have suggested more than once that you write out your philosophy of ministry from the very beginning. If potential members understand that you function as a rancher and are comfortable with it, they will consider joining the church. If not, the best time for them to leave and look for another church is before they join.

Buildings and Bylaws

5. *Facilities*. Start your new church in rented or leased facilities. I do not think I am wrong in saying that the most common conscious decision that church planters have made through the years to lock their church under the 200 barrier is to buy and build too soon. I recommend that you postpone buying land, and especially building as long as you possibly can. In most cases when you first begin thinking, "Maybe it's time to build now," it's probably too soon. Postpone building at least until you are past the 200 barrier with 350 active adults, or better yet 500. If you are like Rick Warren and can grow to over 5,000 before building, do it.

In the last chapter I listed several possible facilities that can be rented or leased. For larger churches the three most feasible may be hotel conference rooms, schools and warehouses. Rick Warren's Saddleback Valley Community Church has grown to 5,000 in schools. John Wimber's Vineyard Christian Fellowship serves a congregation of 6,000 in a renovated warehouse. Warren has purchased land and intends to build, and Wimber is negotiating for permanent facilities at press time.

The larger the congregation, the larger the vision. A congregation of 100 may exercise great faith in raising funds to build a sanctuary for 150 or 200. By doing so they make an architectural statement that they want to be a single cell church. I would guess that nine out of ten churches that build before they cross the 200 barrier never do cross it.

6. *Bylaws*. Try to resist drawing up a full-fledged constitution and bylaws for your church until you have at least

500 members. I know that in some denominations this is impossible. If so you will have to put up with it and make the best of it.

The basic reason for this is that most of the existing traditional models for church constitutions and bylaws tend to siphon off the authority of the pastor and put it in the hands of lay people. Again, I am aware that some subscribe to a philosophy of ministry that sees lay leadership as a biblical mandate. Those, however, who interpret the Bible as centralizing leadership authority in the pastor enjoy a superior growth dynamic. For them it would be well to postpone the constitution and bylaws.

There are some existing models of church constitutions that do centralize leadership in the pastor. Two of which I am aware are the constitution suggested by Elmer Towns in his book *Getting a Church Started*[8] and the model used by the Association of Vineyard Churches. Other independent charismatic churches have similar constitutions, some of which have been criticized for going too far in the other direction and not building in enough accountability for the pastor. There must be a balance of authority and accountability. The general tendency, as history eloquently attests, is that the older a church gets the more the authority tends to be shifted from the pastor to the people.

It is necessary, of course, to fulfill whatever requirements your particular state has for your new church to register as a nonprofit organization. A competent attorney can advise you how to do this with a minimum amount of constitutional bylaws. This will furnish the legal base you need until you decide it is time for the full-fledged constitution.

Thinking Like a Large Church

Carl Dudley has said, "Small is something more than a numerical description." What he means is that smallness is essentially a state of mind. If your goal is for your new church to grow, it must never get itself into the rut of thinking like a small church. Most of the six steps for breaking the 200 barrier listed above will help prevent that. Another list that will be helpful to some is the list of characteristics of a number of prominent churches that have been planted by founding pastors and grown to several thousands in just a few years during the decade of the '80s. Several studies have revealed a profile of these churches that can help you and your people begin thinking like a large church even though there may be only a few people involved at this point:

1. *Conservative theology.* These are mostly evangelical churches with a high view of Scripture and a belief that unbelievers need to be born again or converted.

2. *Strong pastoral leadership.* A rule of thumb is that the larger the church the more crucial is the role of the senior pastor. Even though it is not typical for a smaller church to ascribe a crucial role to the senior pastor, if it wants to grow larger this is one of the first things that must happen.

3. *Participatory worship.* Worship is long (30 to 45 minutes); it features songs written after 1980; there is a freedom for body language through raised hands and other gestures. Contemporary musical instruments are used.

4. *Powerful prayer.* Not only does prayer permeate all aspects of life in these churches, but some have gone so far as to hire full-time, staff-level prayer leaders.

5. *Centrality of the Holy Spirit.* The person and work of the Holy Spirit are stressed. He once again becomes a prominent member of the Trinity, and the works of the Holy Spirit, including supernatural signs and wonders, are welcomed.

6. *Abundant finances.* Through giving and giving generously, the members of these churches have discovered that God loves a cheerful giver and that they cannot outgive God.

7. *Lay ministry.* Each church member is expected to be using his or her spiritual gifts. Many of these churches have developed elaborate and high-quality lay training programs that open the possibility of future ordination to some who are called out of the secular world to full-time ministry.

8. *Life-centered Bible teaching.* Rather than teaching biblical content, the preachers apply biblical teaching to the everyday lives of the church members.

If you apply some or all of these characteristics of rapidly growing churches even in the nucleus building stage, you will release powerful growth dynamics in your new church.

REACHING THE TARGET AUDIENCE

As you reach out to your target audience, you will be at a great advantage if you know ahead of time what their felt needs are. The best way I know of going about this is to use the opinion poll originally suggested by Rick Warren.[9] It is similar to one used previously by Robert Schuller, but the wording is updated. My advice is for the church planter to do this opinion poll and not to delegate it to others. There is no substitute for getting out on the streets yourself and meeting the people firsthand.

Choose 100 households that, so far as you can determine, represent your target audience. Knock on 100 doors at times when people would be expected to be home, but know ahead of time that some of the 100 doors will not open. Ask these five questions, using the exact wording if possible:

WILL YOUR NEW CHURCH GROW? 139

1. Are you an active member of a nearby church? If they are, send greetings to the pastor and move on. You do not want any more information on the needs of Christians. You already know what they are.

2. What do you think is the greatest need among the people of (insert the name of your community)?

3. Why do you think most people around here don't attend church?

4. If you yourself were looking for a church, what kind of things would you look for?

5. What advice would you give me as the pastor of a new church in your community? What specifically could I do for you and your family?

If you carry a clipboard and take notes on each conversation, by the time you finish you will have heard it all over and over again and you will have permanent knowledge of what the needs of the people are. You will know ahead of time that you and your new church can't meet all their needs, but you will identify some that you can meet well. Plug them into your philosophy of ministry.

Move Out Systematically

You and your people have only a limited amount of time to spend on outreach. Therefore you will want to plan to use what time you do have as wisely as possible. Instead of taking a shotgun approach, try to take as much of a rifle approach as possible. Try to use the energy you have available for outreach on those individuals and families whom you can predict will be the most receptive to your message. This does not mean that you wish to bypass or ignore any lost people, but it might well mean that God has prepared you and your people to reach certain segments of the

---

No one can meet everyone's needs. But every church is equipped to meet the needs of some people. Know what your church's strengths are, and play to them.

---

unchurched population while He has called others to reach the rest more effectively than you could do it.

For example, it is worthwhile to dedicate a considerable amount of the time available for outreach to following up the webs of social relationships of those already in your nucleus or in your church. This applies to all your members, but it is especially true of recent converts. The best resource for making this happen is the book by Win and Charles Arn called *The Master's Plan for Making Disciples.*[10] It is important to follow up these webs of relationships as soon as possible after a given individual is either converted or joins the church. If it is not done within a couple of months, the probability of reaching these friends and relatives drops off rapidly.

In addition, locate and spend time with new arrivals in the community. Ask around and find out how to locate those who are just moving in. If you live in Arizona, California, Colorado, Massachusetts, Nevada, New Mexico, Oregon, Utah, or Washington, try getting in touch with the Homeowners Marketing Services, Inc. (12444 Victory Blvd., North Hollywood, CA 91609, 800-232-2134). For a reasonable fee they will provide you once a week with a set of labels giving you the names and addresses of all new home owners in your area. These will be excellent prospects.

Be sure to pay special attention to visitors in your services. Many churches have found them to be the richest source of good prospects for converts and new members. Herb Miller says, "No other single factor makes a greater difference in improving annual membership additions than an immediate visit to the homes of first-time worshipers."[11]

Miller goes on to share some results of his research. He says that if laypeople make 15-minute visits to the homes of those who visit the worship service within 36 hours, 85 percent of them return the following week. If the lag time is 72 hours, the percentage drops to 60, and after one week it drops to 15 percent. Furthermore, if the pastor makes the visit instead of laypeople, the percentage of repeat visits drops in half.[12]

Finally, give high priority to reaching out to those whose needs—whether personal, financial, emotional, vocational, physical, spiritual, or social—you and your church can meet. No one can meet everyone's needs. But every church is equipped to meet the needs of some people. Know what your church's strengths are, and play to them. Robert Schuller's modern-day proverb bears repeating: The secret of success is to find a need and fill it. Often families going through some sort of a life crisis are more open to ministry than at any other time. Births, deaths, divorces, job changes, accidents, financial setbacks, addictions and many other challenges are used by the Holy Spirit to draw people to God.

If you take the pains to know who your target audience is and what their needs are, you can move out with great confidence. There should be no reason why your new church won't grow. My prayer is that it will grow and grow vigorously.

NOTES

1. Paul Yonggi Cho, *Successful Home Cell Groups* (Plainfield, NJ: Logos International, 1981), p. 162.
2. Carl S. Dudley, *Making the Small Church Effective* (Nashville, TN: Abingdon Press, 1978), p. 49.
3. Bill M. Sullivan, *Ten Steps to Breaking the Two Hundred Barrier* (Kansas City, MO: Beacon Hill Press, 1988).
4. Lyle E. Schaller, *The Small Church Is Different* (Nashville, TN: Abingdon Press, 1982), pp. 53-54.
5. I have elaborated on the infrastructure of a growing church including celebration, congregation and cell in my book *Your Church Can Grow* (Ventura, CA: Regal Books, 1979).
6. Wagner, *Leading Your Church to Growth* (Ventura, CA: Regal Books, 1984), p. 79.
7. Elmer Towns, *Getting a Church Started* (Lynchburg, VA: Church Growth Institute, 1985), pp. 123-124.
8. Ibid., pp. 167-175.
9. Rick Warren, *Saddleback Church Growth Lectures* (Mission Viejo, CA: The Encouraging Word, 1982), Tape CG02 "Defined Target."
10. Charles Arn and Win Arn, *The Master's Plan for Making Disciples* (Monrovia, CA: Church Growth).
11. Herb Miller, *How to Build a Magnetic Church* (Nashville, TN: Abingdon Press, 1987), p. 72.
12. Ibid.

RESOURCES FOR CHURCH PLANTERS

Here are the books and other resources on church planting I most highly recommend. Please check the footnotes at the end of each chapter and the bibliography for related resources.

1. Chaney, Charles L. *Church Planting at the End of the Twentieth Century.* Wheaton, IL: Tyndale, 1982. 175 pp. This book takes its place at the top of the list of church planting literature. The material was originally presented as the Church Growth Lectureship at the Fuller Theological Seminary School of World Mission.

2. Durkin, Jim; Dick Benjamin; Larry Tomczak and Terry Edwards. *The Church Planters Handbook.* (Christian Equippers, Box 16100, South Lake Tahoe, CA 95706: 1988.) 170 pp. The four authors tell of the strategies they use to plant churches as apostolic church planters.

3. Falwell, Jerry and Elmer Towns. *Stepping Out on Faith.* Wheaton, IL: Tyndale, 1984, 201 pp. This is a book on faith and church growth. Ten brief case studies of new Liberty Baptist Fellowship churches provide the data base for excellent theorizing on church planting.

144 RESOURCES FOR CHURCH PLANTERS

4. Feeney, James H. *Church Planting by the Team Method.* (Abbott Loop Christian Center, 2626 Abbott Road, Anchorage, AK 99507) 1988, 223 pp. An entire philosophy of church planting by what we call "colonization" is set forth in this book. Many independent charismatic churches are multiplying rapidly by this method.

5. Godwin, David E. *Church Planting Methods.* DeSoto, TX: Lifeshare Communications, 1984, 178 pp. Using evangelistic crusades and supernatural healing in order to plant churches.

6. Hesselgrave, David J. *Planting Churches Cross-Culturally.* Grand Rapids, MI: Baker Book House, 1980. 440 pp. The most complete work in print on E2 and E3 evangelism by one of America's outstanding evangelical missiologists.

7. Logan, Robert E. and Jeff Rast. *Church Planting Workbook* (Charles E. Fuller Institute for Evangelism and Church Growth, Box 91990, Pasadena, CA 91109-1990). Phone: (800) 999-9578. This tool, a fill-in-the-blanks workbook, will take you step-by-step through the process of planning and executing a church planting project. Robert Logan has been actively involved in planting new churches for several years.

8. Logan, Robert E. and Jeff Rast. *Church Planter's Checklist* is a companion to the Church Planting Workbook which will help you systematize and keep track of the successive steps needed to plant the church. Also published by CEFI, and includes 2 cassette tapes by Bob Logan.

9. Shenk, David W. and Ervin R. Stutzman. *Creating Communities of the Kingdom: New Testament Models of Church Planting.* Scottdale, PA: Herald Press. 1988. 229 pp. Of the current books on church planting this one makes the widest use of contemporary resources and state-of-the-art insights. Highly recommended.

10. Starr, Timothy. *Church Planting: Always in Season.* Fellowship of Evangelical Baptist Churches of Canada, 1978. 200 pp. A handbook for church planting which is denominationally oriented but valuable for all.

11. Tinsley, William C. *Upon This Rock: Dimensions of Church Planting.* Atlanta, GA: Baptist Home Mission Board (1350 Spring Street, N.W., Atlanta, GA), 1985. 87 pp. A highly motivational and well written look at church planting from eight different angles. Tinsley combines good research, sharp analysis and practical experience in a strongly recommended book.

12. Towns, Elmer L. *Getting a Church Started.* Privately published in 1982 by the author, but available from the Fuller Seminary Bookstore. This is in the form of a student manual used by Towns at Liberty Baptist Seminary, where church planting is at the heart of the curriculum. It is very practical, and a must for anyone who is or plans to be in the church planting ministry.

13. Wagner, C. Peter. *"How to Plant a Church" Self-Study Pack.* Pasadena, CA: Charles E. Fuller Institute, 1986. The highly successful "How to Plant a Church" seminar lectures have been edited into a self-study packet. The packet contains ten tapes of my church planting lectures and a notebook of self-study material. This is an ideal resource for people wishing to study and review the basic principles of church planting.

14. Warren, Rick. *Saddleback Church Growth Lectures.* Over 11,000 pastors have attended the annual Pastor's Church Growth Conference at Saddleback Valley Community Church. The tapes are a practical and inspirational explanation of Saddleback's strategy for church planting. Write to the Encouraging Word, 24194 Alicia, Suite M, Mission Viejo, CA 92691 or phone 714-587-9534.

BIBLIOGRAPHY

Amberson, Talmadge R., ed. *The Birth of Churches: A Biblical Basis for Church Planting*. Nashville, TN: Broadman Press, 1979.

Appleby, Jerry L. *Missions Have Come Home to America*. Kansas City, MO: Beacon Hill Press, 1986.

Arn, Win and Charles Arn. *The Master's Plan for Making Disciples*. Church Growth, 2670 S. Myrtle Ave., Suite 201, Monrovia, CA 91016.

Benjamin, Dick, Jim Durkin, Terry Edwards, and Larry Tomczak. *The Church Planters Handbook*. Christian Equippers, Int., Box 16100, South Lake Tahoe, CA 95706, 1988.

Bishop, Bryan. "YWAM Steps Out." *World Christian*, January-February, 1986.

Brock, Charles. *The Principles and Practice of Indigenous Church Planting*. Nashville, TN: Broadman Press, 1981.

Carroll, Jackson W. and Robert L. Wilson. *Too Many Pastors?* The Clergy Job Market. New York: The Pilgrim Press, 1980.

Chaney, Charles L. *Church Planting at the End of the Twentieth Century*. Wheaton, IL: Tyndale House, 1982.

Cho, Paul Yonggi. *Successful Home Cell Groups*. Plainfield, NJ: Logos International, 1981.

"Christian Witness to Nominal Christians Among Protestants." Lausanne Occasional Papers No. 23, 1980 (L.C.W.E., Box 1100, Wheaton, IL 60187).

Dorr, Luther M. *The Bivocational Pastor.* Nashville, TN: Broadman Press, 1988.

Dudley, Carl S. *Making the Small Church Effective.* Nashville, TN: Abingdon Press, 1978.

Falwell, Jerry and Elmer Towns. *Stepping Out in Faith.* Wheaton, IL: Tyndale House Publishers, 1984.

Feeney, James H. *Church Planting by the Team Method.* Abbott Loop Christian Center, 2626 Abbott Road, Anchorage, Alaska 99507, 1988.

Goodwin, David E. *Church Planting Methods: A "How-To" Book of Overseas Church Planting Crusades.* Lifeshare Communications, Box 1067, DeSoto, TX 75115, 1984.

Hesselgrave, David J. *Planting Churches Cross-Culturally: A Guide for Home and Foreign Missions.* Grand Rapids, MI: Baker Book House, 1980.

Jones, Ezra Earl. *Strategies for New Churches.* New York, NY: Harper & Row, Publishers, 1976.

Jones, Phil. "An Examination of the Statistical Growth of the Southern Baptist Convention." In *Understanding Church Growth and Decline* 1950-1978, eds. Dean R. Hoge and David A. Roozen. New York: The Pilgrim Press, 1979, p. 170.

Kane, J. Herbert. *The Christian World Mission Today and Tomorrow.* Grand Rapids, MI: Baker Book House, 1981.

Larson, Brian L. *Church Planting Mother-Daughter Style: A Study of Procedures and Results.* D.Min. dissertation, Talbot Theological Seminary, La Mirada, CA, 1984.

Lea, Larry. *Could You Not Tarry One Hour?* Lake Mary, FL: Creation House, 1987.

Logan, Robert E. and Janet Logan. *Spiritual Gifts Implementation.*

Logan, Robert E. *Starting a Church that Keeps on Growing.* The Charles E. Fuller Institute for Evangelism and Church Growth, Box 91990, Pasadena, CA 91109 (800-999-9578), 1986.

McGavran, Donald A and George Hunter III. *Church Growth Strategies that Work.* Nashville, TN: Abingdon Press, 1980.

Merrill, Dean. "Mothering a New Church." *Leadership,* Winter 1985.

Miller, Herb. *How to Build a Magnetic Church.* Nashville, TN: Abingdon Press, 1987.

Peretti, Frank. *This Present Darkness.* Westchester, IL: Crossway Books, 1986.

Platt, Mark. "Church Obstetrics: How a Church Is Born," pamphlet published by Conservative Baptist Association of Northern California, 18510 Prospect Road, Saratoga, CA 95070.

Quinn, Bernard, et al., eds. *Churches and Church Membership in the United States 1980.* Atlanta, GA: Glenmary Research Center, 1982.

Redford, Jack. *Planting New Churches.* Nashville, TN: Broadman Press, 1978.

Ridley, Charles R. *How to Select Church Planters: A Self-Study Manual for Recruiting, Screening, Interviewing, and Evaluating Qualified Church Planters.* Pasadena, CA: Fuller Evangelistic Association, 1988.

Schaller, Lyle E. "Commentary: What Are the Alternatives?" In *Understanding Church Growth and Decline 1950-1978,* ed. Dean R. Hoge and David A. Roozen. New York: The Pilgrim Press, 1979.

Schaller, Lyle E. "Why Start New Churches?" *The Circuit Rider,* May, 1979.

Schaller, Lyle E. *The Small Church Is Different.* Nashville, TN: Abingdon Press, 1982.

Shenk, David W. and Ervin R. Stutzman. *Creating Communities of the Kingdom: New Testament Models of Church Planting.* Scottdale, PA: Herald Press, 1988.

Towns, Elmer. *Getting a Church Started.* Church Growth Institute, Box 4404, Lynchburg, VA 24502, 1985.

Trusty Janice. "The Apprentice Approach." *Missions USA,* January-February, 1983.

Vaughan, John N. *The Large Church.* Grand Rapids, MI: Baker Book House, 1985.

Wagner, C. Peter. *How to Have A Healing Ministry Without Making Your Church Sick.* Ventura, CA: Regal Books, 1988.

————. *Leading Your Church to Growth.* Ventura, CA: Regal Books, 1984.

————. *Your Church Can Be Healthy.* Nashville, TN: Abingdon, 1979.

————. "Evangelizing the Real America." In *The Best in Theology,* Vol. 1, J.I. Packer, ed., Carol Stream, IL: Christianity Today, Inc., 1987.

————. *Your Spiritual Gifts Can Help Your Church Grow.* Ventura, CA: Regal Books, 1979.

Warren, Rick. Saddleback Church Growth Lectures. The Encouraging Word, 24194 Alicia, Suite M, Mission Viejo, CA 92691, 1982, Tape CG02 "Defined Target."

Whan, Norm. *The Phone's for You!* available from Church Growth Development International, 420 W. Lambert, Suite E, Brea, CA 92621 (714-990-9551).

INDEX

Lutheran Church, 31

M
MacArthur, John, 64
Marantika, Christ, 19
Maxwell, John, 49, 54
McClung Jr., Floyd, 23
McAlister, Jack, 22, 23
McKean, Kip, 63
McGavran, Donald A., 41, 46, 65, 75
medicine man, 132
meeting place, 120-122
Melodyland Christian Center, 64
membership decline, 11-12, 17-18, 20, 32, 35
Methodists, 38
Merrill, Dean, 75
Miller, Herb, 141, 142
missionary gift, 67-68
mission team, 70
modality models, 60-69
Mountain View Friends Church, 108
Mount Paran Church of God, 69
multi-congregational model, 67-68
multiple campus model, 68-69

N
name of the church, 118-119
New Life 2000, 24
newspapers, 87
nucleus building, 97-109

O
120 Fellowship, 117-118, 134
Ostling, Richard K., 109
overchurching, 34-35

P
pastoral care, 133-135
Pentecostal movement, 45, 105
People of Destiny International, 74
Perimeter Church, 67
Perkins, Clay, 85
Perretti, Frank, 47, 58
philosophy of ministry, 57, 115-117, 129, 134-135
Piedmont Christian Church, 85
Platt, Mark, 104, 120, 124
Pope, Randy, 67
prayer, 46-51, 102-103, 114-115, 137
prayer, corporate, 48-49
prayer partners, 49-50
PRAXIS Program, 19, 70
preaching, 138
Presbyterian Church of America, 67, 108
Presbyterian Church (USA), 35, 39
public utilities, 85
Putman, Bill, 71

Q
Quinn, Bernard, 95

R
radio stations, 86
Radizeski, Bruno, 102
rancher, 133-135
Rast, Jeff, 109
real estate firms, 87
Redford, Jack, 77, 95
receptivity, 81-82
Reformed Church of America, 118
Regele, Michael B., 88